CW00520916

Awaken the Soul, Release the Spirit

PETER DANBY

THE CHOIR PRESS

Copyright © 2021 Peter Danby

All rights reserved. No part of this publication may be reproduced or
transmitted in any form or by any means, electronic or mechanical including
photocopying, recording or any information storage or retrieval system,
without prior permission in writing from the publishers.

The right of Peter Danby to be identified as the author of this work has
been asserted by him in accordance with the Copyright, Designs and
Patents Act 1988

First published in the United Kingdom in 2021 by
The Choir Press

ISBN 978-1-78963-236-1

Peter Danby was born in 1956 and, after leaving the British Army as a major in 1992, has worked in the areas of leadership development and personal mastery. His work has taken him to 36 countries and many organisations, large and small.

At the heart of his work is deep sense of a spiritual impulse, a calling to bring an awareness of the many dimensions of our nature into the world. Inspired by his grandmother, he trained as a healer, as a Reiki master and entered a mystical school to explore the hidden realms. It was here that he was challenged to become the 'mystic in the marketplace'; living the philosophy rather than withdrawing to a monastery or mountain retreat.

Today, Peter's work also involves young people in Sri Lanka, Nepal, Rwanda and refugees in Greece. This book is an attempt to bring together his experiences in a way that will enable others to discover, explore and live full and fulfilling lives.

He lives in Kent with his wife, Rosy.

Contents

Oriah Mountain Dreamer for 'The Invitation'
Sassoon

The Invitation. By 'Oriah Mountain Dreamer' taken from her
book 'The Invitation' © 1999. Published by HarperOne,
San Francisco.

All rights reserved. Presented with permission of the author
www.oriah.org.

Extracts from the poem 'The Aftermath' copyright Siegfried
Sassoon with permission kindly granted by the Estate of
George Sassoon.

Awakening the Soul

SETTING THE SCENE

So, who is this book for? My answer is very simple. It is for whomever has come to be reading these words. You may be exploring spirituality for the first time, or have been searching all your life. You may be disillusioned or dissatisfied with formal religion, with your life as it is now or the state of the world. You may even have picked up the book by mistake but, if you stay and keep reading, then I am writing for you. My aim is to introduce a way for each of us who is ready to discover, explore and then express the spiritual impulse within. I want you to come on a journey with me, and I could not find any better way of expressing the invitation to you than in the following passage.

The Invitation

It doesn't interest me what you do for a living. I want to know what you ache for, and if you dare to dream of meeting your heart's longing.

It doesn't interest me how old you are. I want to know if you will risk looking like a fool for love, for your dreams, for the adventure of being alive . . .

It doesn't interest me what planets are squaring your moon. I want to know if you have touched the centre of your own sorrow, if you have been opened by life's betrayals or have become shrivelled and closed from fear of further pain. I want to know if you can be with joy, mine or your own; if you can dance with wildness and let the ecstasy fill you to the tips of your fingers and toes without cautioning us to be careful, be realistic, or to remember the limitations of being human.

1 want to know if you can see beauty even when it is not pretty every day, and if you can source your life from its own presence. I want to know if you can live with failure, yours and mine, and still stand on the shore of a lake and shout to the silver of a full moon 'YES!'

It doesn't interest me who you are, how you came to be here. I want to know if you will stand in the centre of the fire with me and not shrink back.

It doesn't interest me where or what or with whom you have studied. I want to know what sustains you from the inside when all else fails away. I want to know if you can be alone with yourself, and if you truly like the company you keep in the empty moments.

From Oriah Mountain Dreamer, Native Elder, May 1994

An Old Story

There is a lovely, old story about a village in the hill country of a remote land, which had a beautiful golden statue of the Buddha. When the villagers heard that a foreign army was about to invade their village, they covered the statue with dirt and mud, altering the shape and hiding the gold so that it would not be stolen. The statue survived the invasion and the many subsequent years of foreign rule. Indeed, by the time the invaders left, the local population had forgotten the origins of the statue and no longer worshipped beside it or cared for it. Until, one day, a piece of mud and dirt broke away and revealed the gold underneath to the delighted villagers.

Inspired by the discovery, the villagers took time away from their work to scrape and clean the statue and reveal the beautiful gold from which the statue was formed. Once again, it became the centre of village life.

The Awakening

Like all good stories, there is a metaphor and a lesson. The story is the story of our lives. When we are born, we are pure gold – untainted and connected to the pure consciousness from whence we came. Then, as we go through life, we lose our innocence and purity and we are covered with the 'mud' – the need to conform to all the social influences around us – hiding our true, golden nature. We are taught to value power over others, we are encouraged to 'win at all costs', we are expected to conform to the wishes of our parents, priests and teachers or behave so we gain the approval of our peers. At some stage, though, there will be some event in our lives that will shake and crack that covering shell. Perhaps a loss, an accident or illness. Perhaps, even, a film or book to bring a new awareness. Then, if we are fortunate or if we look hard enough, we will see that there is something more to us than this covering of cultural conformity. Then, if we are prepared to spend time and effort in clearing away the clouds that have gathered over our souls, we can reconnect with the source and that pure consciousness. I hope that this book may be a moment of discovery or a re-awakening.

The Hero's Journey

In his book *The Hero with a Thousand Faces*, Joseph Campbell describes the origins and power of storytelling, and one archetypal story common to every culture in our world: the hero's journey. Many great films, great fictional books will follow a pattern; the hero or heroine is taken from, or leaves, their safe existence and sets out on a quest or a challenge. In this 'new, darker world' they will travel long and far, face great tasks and slay dragons, they will find new skills and talents and meet wise old men or women to help them on their way. Then, finally, when they have fulfilled their quest, they face the final hurdle, to cross the threshold back to this world, bringing their new talents and gifts. That archetypal story is our story; we are the hero or the heroine and the journey is the potential story of our life. It is the story of us breaking out of that cloak of mud and our safe, conforming existence and seeking the gold within. The challenges represent the challenges we face in our life and the dragons are the doubts and fears that hold us back. The archetypal story works so well because it touches something deep within us and draws us into the narrative.

Let me give you just one example. When the film *The Shawshank Redemption* was released in 1994 it was a box-office disappointment. Since then, it has become rated by many sources as one of the greatest movies ever made. Why? Of course, there is great acting and screenplay but the real reason is that it is a classic hero's journey story, beautifully told. An accountant is ripped out of his safe existence and imprisoned. In prison, this dark underworld, he faces many challenges and uses his talents and courage to overcome them. He meets a wise old man to help him on his journey and then, when he has overcome his dragons, his final challenge is to cross the threshold back into the world, to escape the prison and bring us the gifts of hope and freedom. Like all great stories, it captures our soul – it touches the hero or the heroine within us.

The Call to Arms – Searching for the soul, the gold within

I am asking you to shed the cloak of mud that surrounds you, and to journey to seek the gold that lies within. To awaken the soul and release the spirit. In our modern society - perhaps throughout our history - our souls have been much neglected. We have worked hard to create a world full of bright, shiny inventions. We honour the intellect and we measure success and achievement in material wealth, academic prowess, fame and power. Those values have led us to impose a deep suffering on the natural world around us and to a constant state of conflict with, and violence towards, each other. We must break those chains and find a way to connect to our 'golden' nature.

THE PATH OF THE MYSTIC

The Chains That Bind Us

Throughout human history, in our drive for order and control we have created a web of binding cultural structures and systems. Our spiritual life has suffered from the same drive. How easy it is for the original teachings of the prophets and seers to be transformed into a doctrine, a structure and a system which demands conformity and submission. For an individual to lose sight of their own true nature and give up the responsibility for their own development, expression and growth. How easy it is for the hierarchy of the religion to become just another way to gain power over others.

To know ourselves as we truly are, as part of the great flow and expression of life, of all that is, has become the domain of the hermit, the New Age traveller or weird ascetic in the desert. Yet we all have very different lives and challenges to face. We have different physical bodies and vastly different environments to grow up in. It is hardly surprising that religions, which attempt to build a common template for our divine experience and channel us along a pre-determined path, do not fulfil everybody's needs.

Light and Shadow in Religion

There is much we can take from formal religion. It brings us into a relationship with our fellow men and fellow women, as well as with the higher dimensions. There are great benefits in a shared set of values and the social order and balance that comes from their disciplined application. Great works can and have been done by religious communities.

The shadow, though, is long and dark. Our need to belong and a fear of death makes us vulnerable to those who claim divine authority. Power seduces and corrupts and it is too easy for the essence of a religion to be lost as its members focus more on power games and personal agendas than the original teachings. Too often, the willingness to conform and submit has led to the giving up of our individual responsibility, to fanaticism and all the brutal acts that spring from it.

Another Way

There is another way: to walk our own path rather than follow others. To experience a personal relationship with the Creative Source rather than receive it through a pre-ordained format. To take responsibility for our own spiritual growth rather than abdicate it to somebody else, whatever robes they might wear or staffs of authority they might carry.

The Path of the Mystic

This is the path of the mystic. Mysticism is, essentially, the pursuit of a personal experience with your divine nature, your innermost truth, with what some might call God. The intimacy you may experience is a 'knowing', which goes beyond and above all beliefs and identities and so does not need to be based on a cult or a religion. Our modern world encourages a self-seeking path, a quest for material wealth and glory without concern for the damage done to others or the world. The mystic walks a different path. Connecting to the pure consciousness at our centre, to the 'oneness' of which we are a part, automatically leads us onto a path based on the 'higher' human values of love, kindness, generosity and service.

Who Walks This Path?

The title of mystic isn't something just reserved for saints or gurus. It is the choice of any individual to have that divine revelation and communion with the Creative Source. Nor is it something that is only found in the mountains of Tibet, on a pilgrimage, by spending long years in the desert or studying with a guru in India. Mysticism is primarily an inner journey and the path that this journey follows is the experience of your own life, wherever you are and whoever you are with. Of course, solitude is useful for certain disciplines, but we learn about ourselves through the lessons that the world places before us. In the turmoil of daily life in the city, there are a thousand such lessons for us. What is needed is the awareness and understanding to recognise and interpret them, then the discipline to apply them in our lives.

How Do I Learn to Walk This Path?

There are mystical schools and I certainly gained invaluable guidance from mine, White Lodge. The teachers and teachings are there, though, to broaden the horizons of our own thinking and not stifle it with a rigid doctrine. The only entry qualification is an open and enquiring mind. There are many guides and you may have found one here. We all teach to the level of our own understanding and, when you are ready, you will find another - and perhaps become one yourself. When you do, be guided by these beautiful words written by a young Chilean schoolboy. They were written for his school teachers; they could have been written as a manifesto for spiritual teachers.

Don't impose on me what you know
I want to explore the unknown
And be the source of my own discoveries
Let the known be my liberation, not my slavery

The world of your truth can be my limitation;
Your wisdom my negation
Don't instruct me, let's walk together
Let my richness begin where yours ends

Show me that I can stand on your shoulders
Reveal yourself so that I can be something different

You believe that every human being
Can love and create
I understand then, your fear
When I ask you to live, according to your wisdom

You will not know who I am
By listening to yourself
Don't instruct, let me be
Your failure is that I am identical to you

Umberto Maturana

A Lonely Path – but you are never alone

The mystic's path is a magical path, but it can also be lonely - few people in the world as it is now will understand where you are going and why. Fewer still will know what it is that you talk of when you do experience that inner knowing. There are, though, always good souls around us to provide support. So, when we need to, we connect with others, not to form another institution with all the hierarchies, politics and pressures, but to provide support and encouragement for each other. Perhaps, together, we can encourage others to break the chains too, and release their spirit into our world.

MY JOURNEY

I have always been encouraged to teach from my own experience so I will tell you something of my own journey and then introduce you to the teachings that have influenced me. It may reassure you to find out that I have no special psychic talents, have heard no voices from another world or seen a great light in the sky. We do not need those things to walk this path. Before I begin though, I want you to listen to the advice of the Buddha who said:

Do not believe in what you have heard; do not believe in traditions because they have been handed down for many generations; do not believe in anything because it is rumoured and spoken by many; do not believe merely because a written statement of some old sage is produced; do not believe in conjectures; do not believe in that as truth to which you have become attached from habit; do not believe merely the authority of your teachers and elders. After observation and analysis, when it agrees with reason and is conducive to the good and gain of one and all, then accept it and live up to it.

This is wonderful advice for our modern world: all the information, ideas and news - or is it fake news? Test all that you hear, not just from me but whatever or whoever the source, against your own logic, your own experience and your own intuition.

The Early Years

My first memory of an experience which I might call spiritual was when I was seven years old. In our primary school class, we had morning prayers with a hymn and a bible reading. It was my turn to do the reading and I remember reading the passage, describing how

> *'It is easier for a camel to pass through the eye of a needle than for a rich man to enter the kingdom of God.'*
>
> Luke 18:25.

When I finished the reading, I was meant to sit down and wait for the teacher to announce the hymn. I didn't do that and I remember continuing by saying, 'Of course, you know that it is not some rich man Jesus is talking about; it is us – it is you and I. We live in a rich world and have forgotten how to live a spiritual life.' I can also remember the look of disbelief on the face of my teacher as she heard this little boy, who had yet to travel beyond the rolling countryside of North Devon, delivering his insight on our world. My only interests at that time were playing football and climbing trees and, if you had asked me where those words came from, I would be as dumbfounded as she was. As I look back, with my understanding of the idea of reincarnation, of our living many lives, I can't help but think that those words came from a deep, unconscious part of my being.

My maternal grandmother was, what was then known as, a faith healer. She attended spiritualist churches where messages were received from the spirit world and she could see and read the aura. I have never needed to hear any scientific evidence of 'other worlds'. I experienced her healing and her psychic talents and I grew up accepting the multi-dimensional layers of our existence as very normal. Nana had once said to me during a healing session, 'You know that you can do this too, you are a healer.' So, when I left the army back in 1992, I set our to find out what lay behind her words. I trained to become a healer and began to explore those 'other dimensions'. My search continues as I try to hold the balance between being open to new experience and understanding while testing it all with my logic and a critical, discerning eye.

The Army – a spiritual training ground

I still find it of great interest that some of the best training for my spiritual life came in my army days, training to fight. A few years ago now, a wonderful friend and colleague asked me, 'Did you have to unlearn a lot when you left the army?' My answer to her was, 'Actually, no. My challenge has been to try to remember all the lessons and how I learnt or was taught.' Those lessons were about self-discipline, resilience and focus. You are often put under pressure or in hostile situations where it is easy to allow the emotions to take over. Yet, for survival and also to fulfil the responsibility of the soldier and the use of arms within society, you have to learn how to master those emotions and choose the right course of action. The motto of the Royal Military Academy is 'Serve to Lead' and I learnt hard lessons about my responsibility, as an officer, to serve my soldiers. I learnt lessons about meaning and purpose at every level. It was an incredible education and I still seek ways to bring some of those lessons into my own work.

Stepping Off the Ledge

As I was leaving the army, I met an inspiring woman who was running her own business. I was hoping to get some insights into the secret of setting up a business but, instead, she gave me something much more precious. It was another story. She had encouraged her staff to put together a beautiful little book of inspirational quotes and stories. She had drawn her own stories from the book, *Jonathon Livingstone Seagull*, and they inspired me to read the book. It is a story of a seagull who loved to explore the joys of flight and of life. He refused to be constrained by the rules and the doctrine of the flock, eventually being forced to leave the flock so that he could explore the fullness of life. Through his experiences, he met guides who helped him reach a higher level of consciousness and then return to the flock as a teacher, to encourage other gulls to expore and learn for themselves. The seagull is on the front cover of my journal and a constant reminder of my own quest.

Deep Memories

Over the years, travelling to many countries and meeting a number of gifted mediums, I have built a strong sense of a soul that has lived many lives. From the forests in Washington State in America, to the caves around Qumran in Israel, I have experienced intense memories rising, unbidden from within. As I mentioned, there has been no blinding flash of light, no voices speaking to me from the heavens – much as I have hoped for such revelations. My journey on this higher path, as I describe it, has been slow and steady. I have enjoyed studying the rich variety of spiritual maps, ancient and modern, from around the world and always tried to stay open to deeper levels of understanding.

Guidance on the Journey

Do you ever get that feeling of being gently guided to where you need to be? It's always interesting to look back and reflect on all those 'sliding door' moments in your life – the people you have met, the choices you made and the events you have been part of. Almost as I began training to be a healer I found a spiritual centre just a couple of miles from our new home. I first went to this centre, White Lodge, in 1992 and began a ten-year initiation into a mystical school founded by a teacher called Ronald Beesley. When I was training in the healing art of Reiki a few years later, my teacher at our first meeting, before I had given her any of my background, asked me if I knew Ronald Beesley, as he was watching closely over me – as he had in previous lives. It sounds weird to many, I know, but when something like that happens, it does make you stop and think. Well, it did that for me.

In the same way that I was drawn to White Lodge I have the sense of having been trained in a particular way through my life and for a particular role. I have followed my own path, sometimes when it seemed crazy to do so, but, looking back, it has always felt as though I have been put in the right places at the right time to do this work.

The Mystic in the Marketplace

William Lambert, one of my spiritual teachers, introduced me to the idea of the 'mystic in the marketplace'. In previous lives, perhaps, the spiritual path involved withdrawing from society and living in a monastery or in some isolated cave. Our role now, though, he told us, is to bring that spiritual dimension into our everyday lives. I decided that the best way to use my talents to heal and to teach was through my work in leadership development; encouraging young people in particular, to lead by inspiring, enabling and encouraging rather than through authority and power. In 2004, I began to run a spiritual workshop at London Business School, introducing managers to mindfulness, meditation and other practices. In 2009, I set up a charity and now run projects in Nepal, Sri Lanka and Rwanda, bringing together my experience in leadership development, my love of sport and my desire to serve others. I see that my challenge now is to draw on the wisdom of the great souls, maintain the essence and purity of their teachings and the vibration, but in a way that will meet the needs of those I work with.

Still Flying

I wrote this little poem when I was in the process of leaving the army. It seemed a big step at the time and you can see the influence of Jonathon Livingstone in there. Looking back, I see that all I was doing was following my true nature – the spirit within.

Take the Step
Peter Danby 1992

To be all you can be you must dream to be more.
To achieve all that is possible, you must attempt the impossible.
So, look to the skies, step off the ledge and fly free,
Where the only limits are those you set yourself;
Where you may soar as high as you dare, and then go higher.
Take courage, be true to yourself, take the step ...

I am still flying and still blessed to be meeting new guides who lift me higher. Still open to exploring new horizons and testing the limits.

The Magic and Beauty of the Mystic's Path

I wrote some words for my beautiful little granddaughter back in 2019. The message was very personal but, as I re-read the words, I feel that they capture so much of what I would like to impart through my teaching work. So, with one or two small alterations, I want to share them with you. Mingled in with my own words are exerts from two wonderful pieces. The first is 'My Law' which is attributed to a Maori and you can read in full a little later. Second, a poem by Paramahamsa Satyananda Saraswati about what it means to be a Sannyasin. A Sannyasin is an ascetic, a person who renounces material desires and prejudices, adopts an attitude of detachment from material life, and has the purpose of spending their life in a peaceful, love-inspired, simple spiritual life. I am not suggesting that we move into a cave or become a hermit, but it illustrates something of the nature of this higher path. I have called my words 'My Blessing'.

MY BLESSING

What can I possibly say to you that might be of some use and guidance? Your path will be so different to my own.

So, what I will say comes from the heart, for I can boast no great intellect or psychic talents. These words come from my own living experience, from a sense of a deep knowing about life, about who we are and why we are here.

In your heart and soul, you hold a precious seed of light, it is the essence of life itself. The world and people will swirl around you like shadows across the sun, but this part of you is timeless, indestructible; it holds the lessons from the past and all that you have become. It is your true nature.

You were. You will be! Know this while you are:
Your spirit has travelled both long and far.
It came from the Source, to the Source it returns –
The Spark which was lighted eternally burns.

It slept in a jewel. It leapt in a wave.
It roamed in the forest. It rose from the grave.
It took on strange garbs for long eons of years
And now in the soul of yourself it appears.

Even in the dark moments, and there will be such times, hold to this centre; learn to listen to the quiet voice of your soul. It links you to those souls around you who will love and watch over you - and we will be there too. It links you to your eternal self and to the great source from which you were born.

You are an invisible child of a thousand faces of love that floats over the swirling sea of life, surrounded by the meadows of winged shepherds, where divine love and beauty, the stillness of midnight summer's warmth pervades.

Life will bring you many experiences and, from all of them - the good and the not so good - you can learn; that is why we are here, to develop the soul. But, be sure, you will face nothing that you are not strong enough to deal with. Always you will have the choice of how to face these experiences, be they joyful or harsh and we can only urge you not to turn from them. Stay true to your own values and what you know in your heart to be 'the right thing'. Live life to the full, treat each breath, each moment as a gift from the gods; it is.

I shall be a witness, but never shall I run or turn from life, from me. Never shall I forsake myself or the timeless lessons that I have learnt. Nor shall I let the value of divine inspiration and being be lost. My rainbow-covered bubble will carry me further than beyond the horizons, forever to serve, to love and to live.

There are some simple questions to ask yourself as you walk this path; they will help guide your steps. What experiences do you wish to have? How do you wish to grow - in mind, body and spirit? What will you contribute to the world around you - what talents do you have and how can you best use them to serve? Through these questions you will come to find your soul purpose and, when you

do, strive with all your might to achieve it. Don't wait for the world
to bring these gifts to you.

*Shall I fall on bended knee and wait for someone to bless me
with happiness and a life of golden dreams? No, I shall run into
the desert of life with my arms open, sometimes falling,
sometimes stumbling, but always picking myself up, a
thousand times if necessary, sometimes happy. Often life will
burn me, often life will caress me tenderly and many of my
days will be haunted with complications and obstacles and
there will be moments so beautiful that my soul will weep
in ecstasy.*

The world is full of beauty and grace. The world is full of brutality
and darkness. Be aware of your own humanity; never forget that we
are divine beings living within the physical body of an animal, with
animal instincts and drives. We all hold the seed of light and love and
we all hold the seed of violence and darkness. Feed and nurture the
one that you wish to live within you. Our world is what we have
chosen to make it and our future is what we choose it to be. As long
as you listen to your heart, live with love, seek to serve then you can
know that your soul will sing with joy and the angels will sing with
you.

Walk freely but with a care. There are many wonderful, sacred
scripts that can help guide us. Read them, meditate on them, but do
not be bound by any one belief. There are many 'false prophets' and
tricksters who will seek to win your trust; be careful of them. Test
everything that you read, see or hear against your own logic, your
own inner guide.

*You are your own Devil, you are your own God
You fashioned the paths your footsteps have trod.
And no one can save you from Error or Sin
Until you have hark'd to the Spirit within.*

May your life be a long, full and happy one. May you discover and fully express the talents that you have and may you know the joy of using them in the service of others. May you love passionately and deeply and may you always know that you are loved and watched over, in this life and the next.

With my love and blessing,
Peter

The Dangers and Darkness

I look at the whole history of humanity and recognise that my dream of creating a future where we live in a fair, just, equitable and peaceful world is an endless battle in which I have chosen to fight. I love the irony of that; fighting for peace.

History also shows the dangers of trying to bring about change in an existing system, whether in nature or in society, however good the intentions. Libya and Iraq are recent examples. Yet the mystic's path challenges much of what our current world holds dear and will fight to maintain. I seek to change the way we live. Not by imposing a new system or structure but by lifting our individual and collective consciousness. Why? Partly because I like a challenge. Partly because, at this point in our history, I think it is more important than ever for each one of us to choose, consciously, to live in a different way. Let me explain by describing how recent world events, as well as history, have shaped my thinking.

THE WORLD WE LIVE IN

Will it Ever Change?

It was back in 2016 and I had just returned from Rwanda, where I was running a leadership programme for young students. I stayed in Nyamata, a small town to the south of Kigali, and while I was there I visited a church near my hotel, which has been converted into a genocide memorial. In April to July 1994, 10,000 Tutsi men, women and children came to this place of refuge, this holy place, only to be slaughtered – with guns, with fire and with machetes – inside the walls. In all, some 50,000 lie buried in the grounds. Then, on the last day of my visit, I walked around the national genocide memorial in Kigali with the friend who had brought me to Rwanda. Over 250,000 are buried there. My friend was just seven years old when he lost his entire family in the killings, and I could not bring myself to look at his face as we read, heard and saw the stories of neighbours killing neighbours, of the inhumanity that swept this beautiful country of a thousand hills.

Back home from that trip, in the summer, I captained my village cricket team in our annual memorial game with the Siegfried Sassoon Fellowship. A son of the village, Siegfried was one of the great war poets and, after winning a Military Cross, spoke out strongly against the conduct of the war. Each year I read one of his poems at the end of the game, it's called 'The Aftermath' and contains a heart-wrenching message. Below are some of the words from his poem.

Have you forgotten yet? ...? For the world's events have rumbled on since those gagged days ... Look down, and swear by the slain of the War that you'll never forget ... Do you remember the rats; and the stench of corpses rotting in front of the front-line trench- ... And dawn coming, dirty-white, and chill with a hopeless rain? ... Do you ever stop and ask, 'Is it all going

19

*to happen again?' Have you forgotten yet? ... ? **Look up, and swear by the green of the spring that you'll never forget.***

In that summer, with the death of some 800,000 Tutsis fresh in my mind, we remembered the hundredth anniversary of the Battle of the Somme, where some 800,000 died in the beautiful French countryside. As I was reading reports from around the world – Syria, Yemen, Afghanistan, Libya – I could feel my spirit sinking further into a dark abyss as I reflected on how little we have changed in the last hundred, thousand or ten thousand years. And, finally, in my own country, the 'United' Kingdom, it was the time of the Brexit referendum: the beginning of one of the most divisive periods in our history, shattering the bonds which have held us together as a nation and perhaps even taking us to more conflict with our neighbours – again. So, I wrote this:

THE CHOICE

Will it ever end:
The lies, the treachery, the selfish greed and lust for power?
Will it ever end:
The abuse, the endless quest for more, for bigger, for better
than you?

No, my friend, it will never end.
Always the race begins again as soon as the killing ceases
Vengeance calls before the blood has soaked away.
The young prepare for battle as the already old weep.

So why even start,
When we know our dreams must fade?
Why start afresh, why bother at all,
When the sands we build on are shifting still?

Why? Because that is who we are. That is life.
The acorn sprouts as the old oak dies.
Ashes to ashes as the new babe cries.
Love and hate; the endless cycle of life.

Within each of us sits light and darkness.
We all know anger, we all feel joy.
We can all hate and we can all forgive
It is for us to choose.

As some will build, so some destroy.
There is no right without wrong.
There is no love without hate.
It is for us to choose.

So, we try do what is right,
Not what others do.
We try to live with love, not hate.
We try to forgive and judge only our self.

Hold back the need to wound or kill.
Hold back the words that cut and hurt.
Pick up the pieces and begin again.
Heal the wounds and rebuild afresh.

No, it will never end.
The great circle of life; light and darkness need each other.
Just choose the light. Be the light.
It is the right thing to do, nothing more. Make the right choice.

I know that my words, my actions, my life will have little impact on
the future of our species. However, I know that it is important for
me to try; to choose a different path and speak, act and live in a way
that reflects the part of our nature that lifts us beyond the animal. It

is important too, for me to try to encourage others to follow that path.

Knowledge is Not Enough – A new leadership is needed

The original and untainted teachings of the great masters are still as relevant today as they were thousands of years ago – so why does nothing change? The challenge is not to know how to live in harmony together, the challenge is for enough of us to act on that knowledge, for long enough to change the patterns of thinking that shape our world.

It is those patterns that I seek to challenge and break, and it will not happen by creating new systems, new religions or institutions. It will happen when each one of us awakens the soul, discovers the gold within and chooses to live a more mindful, purposeful and fulfilling life. It will happen when the leaders of our communities and organisations, at every level, lead with an awareness and understanding of our whole self and the true purpose of life.

THIS RETREATING WORLD

Wilfred Owen, another war poet, in his poem 'Strange Meeting' suggests that, in our vanity, we think we are constantly progressing and have created a great society. Sitting in the mud and excrement, the blood and filth of his trench, it is not hard to see how that illusion of progress faded like a mirage.

Our Hubris

As we have become more and more connected through our city life and our incredible communication systems, we have become more and more disconnected from the world around us. We have never been so rich or knowledgeable, yet never more polarised in our societies. We have achieved astonishing advances in science and our understanding of the world around us and yet poverty, fanaticism, violence and the abuse of power are as prevalent as they ever were. For all our talk of progress, we are no closer to mastering our instinctive nature and creating a society built on the values of our higher self or soul. Fairness and social responsibility rather than personal agendas, ambition, strength and power.

Heading in the Wrong Direction

Progress has come to mean higher targets, bigger cars, bigger buildings, more production, profit and material wealth. The rules of the 'real world' are that, if you work harder than others and strive to outperform them, you will be successful and this will lead to happiness. The results of this mindset are there for us all to see; we are destroying our planet and ourselves.

All the spiritual paths suggest there is more to life than material wealth. Many of them suggest that the purpose of life is development and growth of a different kind, of the soul. That the measure of our work, our success and our life is our state of being, of our consciousness ... right here, right now. Yet, despite the work and teachings of the great religions – sometimes because of them – we continue to fight. We continue to rape our planet and violate so many forms of life on our shared world. We seem unable to learn how to evolve, to move forward and break out of the endless cycle of violence. To change, we need to step off the path we are chasing down and choose another way. So easy to say, seemingly impossible to do.

Breaking the Chains

It is seductively easy to follow the directions and expectations of the crowd, or of those with the power to influence or dictate - social media, businesses and politicians. We can continue arguing, fighting and even killing others over which is the right path to take. We can 'rage against the machine' and demand that those in power make the changes we crave. Or, we can begin to act in a different way. We can simply stop trying to persuade others or attach ourselves to the ways of others and follow our own path, taking responsibility for our own life. We can do this, even when we know that others, especially those with power, will cling to those old patterns. The alternative is to remain in the continuous cycle of suffering and violence that now threatens our very existence on this planet.

Does It Matter?

Does any of this matter in the great scheme of things? I have an understanding that our souls have lived many lives, and in each life we can learn and evolve. Even in a world of darkness, it can be argued that our souls have learnt from the abuse, the violence and the suffering. Today though, as our current way of living rushes us towards an environmental disaster, perhaps to the extinction of all life on our Mother Earth, there is an additional incentive to change our way of life and walk another path: to maintain all life on our planet.

That has set the scene for my book. We are nearly ready to begin our journey.

Exploring and Discovery

I find it interesting that, as children, we are never taught the most important skill that we need in life: how to learn. Even more important if we are to fulfil our purpose in this life: how to learn from our own life, from our lived experience and from life itself. There is another challenge too, in that much of this journey of discovery is an inner journey, exploring the depths of our being, and there are few schools around the world that encourage this kind of learning.

So, before we begin to explore, I would like to take some time to introduce you to two practices that have been at the heart of my own spiritual journey.

THE 4ᵀᴴ SPACE

The idea of the 4th Space was born in 2004: my final project on a postgraduate programme at University of Surrey. The programme was called Spiritual Development and Facilitation and the focus of the final module challenged us to take the spiritual dimension into our work place. I accepted the challenge and decided to see if I could run a spiritually-based workshop at London Business School, with its reputation for rigorous scientific research, for finance and strategy. You can probably imagine the reaction when I proposed the idea to some of the professors, although they did me the honour of listening to my proposal. Despite the clear lack of scientific rigour and research, I found a way to run a workshop called the 4th Space. It ran successfully as a part of one of the school's flagship executive education programmes for 15 years before budget cuts finally ended it.

The 4th Space is an idea that has brought together some of the different threads of my life: leadership, personal mastery, teaching and my work in the business world. Business schools and leadership development programmes do a great job at covering the physical, mental and emotional dimensions of leadership, but I wanted to address the spiritual dimension – not a common area of study in our modern, profit-driven business world. At the very heart of my leadership philosophy is, quite simply, the quality and essence of your being.

The inspiration for the name originally came from Starbucks, the coffee shop. They used the expression 'the third space' – a place to socialise – to describe their coffee shops. The first and second spaces being our home and work. I wanted to create a fourth space, a space you withdraw or 'retreat' to with the specific aim of nurturing those inner qualities and the higher dimensions of ourselves. It is a time and place of stillness, for meditation, for reflection and deep contemplation. It is a time and space for reconnecting with the deepest part of your being, your soul or spirit and for gathering energy and restoring balance; the 'eye of the storm', the pause before the action begins again.

The 4th Space might be a time of the day when you step back from the swirling pressures of the world, or a longer period when you 'retreat' from that world to travel an inner journey. It also represents the space between the thought and the action in the middle of a meeting or the heat of a conflict, the space we create to detach, manage our emotions and make the right choice of words and actions. So, it is a time and space but also an attitude, an approach that enables the development of these higher dimensions and a way of life that springs from them.

Spending time in the 4th Space can help us re-energise physically, emotionally and mentally through practices such as mindfulness, meditation and contemplation.

It can be a space where we reconnect with our sense of purpose and where we can listen to our intuition, or let our imagination and creative talents run free.

Try making the 4th Space a part of your daily life. There will always be things going on around you which will demand your attention, but if you do not create this 4th Space and dedicate this time for your inner work, then you will remain as you are, blown this way and that by the winds of the world. Developing yourself and following a spiritual path requires discipline and new practices. The 4th Space is a way of bringing that discipline and those practices into your life.

THE DISCIPLINE OF LEARNING

A New Goal for Learning

What could be more important than our ability to learn if the purpose of life is the education of the soul? Not learning a new skill, but learning to evolve our state of being or consciousness. I am going to suggest that you place the discipline of learning at the heart of your life.

Progress, for me, is not the size of our bank account, our house or car. It is measured by the quality of our being, our physical, mental, emotional and spiritual equilibrium. We progress as we learn. Not in the conventional way of learning – by reading books or being taught – but from our own experience, from our own life.

The University of Life

'I studied at the "University of Life".' I remember it was a favoured expression in the days when university was the domain of the select few. And yet, it holds so much truth for me. Life, if we are open to it, brings us a never-ending series of challenges and opportunities from which we can learn. It is more than just the development of new skills and behaviours or about the achievement of a specific goal – it is a growing consciousness. You discover and learn how to express your whole self – with awareness and skill.

> *'If you can meet with triumph and disaster,*
> *And treat these twin imposters just the same'*
> Rudyard Kipling 'If'

The Learning Mentality

By adopting a learning mentality, we nurture a sense of humility which impacts on our relationship with people and the world around us. We move beyond that fragile and superficial measure of success – 'triumph and disaster' – and begin to experience a growing sense of inner confidence in our ability to cope with whatever life throws at us. It gives us a new perspective, a sense of detachment, which enables us to regulate our emotions more effectively. Lao Tzu called this ability to detach and live with this perspective the primal virtue. It nurtures a positive outlook and brings us closer to true, unconditional happiness.

The Learning Process

We learn from experience, reflection, contemplation and meditation. It is not an easy path. Learning and development in any walk of life requires purposeful practice – and discipline. We need to be open to change and to feedback. We need to be mindful of our mental blocks and fears and, we need to be disciplined and have the will to implement our plans. Developing a new skill or behaviour requires cycle after cycle of practice and review. In Tai Chi, it is said that to master a new movement or technique requires the student to hold it in the conscious mind for 100 days. The principle is a good one – once again, development of any kind requires discipline.

The Learning Cycle

One of my inspirations in this field is David Kolb. In his learning cycle, he describes how our learning as adults starts with an experience. We have many experiences, of course, but just having the experience doesn't guarantee that we learn from it. Indeed, it is an interesting exercise to look back at 'repeated mistakes' and to see how many times we go from one 'bad' experience to another without learning from either. Not just bad experiences either. It is too easy to win a game or to gain a success in any arena and see it as a sign of our natural talent or simply good fortune – and not learn from the experience.

Kolb recognises four stages of learning (having an experience, processing what happened, drawing lessons from it and then planning how to apply those lessons). In the right-hand diagram below, they are seen here as a continuous cycle or spiral of learning – highlighting its continuous nature.

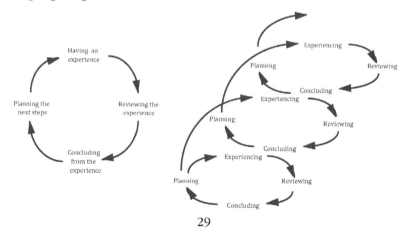

The Many Levels of Learning

Learning is complex and takes place at many levels. There is a flow between the inner and outer world - each impacting on the other. Our inner voice ('I can't do this') or deep memories can be a block to learning that is nothing to do with actual ability. On the positive side, conquering fearful challenges in the outer world can impact on the beliefs that you have about yourself and your potential. At the physical, business-oriented level, this manifests in increased efficiency and higher levels of performance. At deeper levels, it moves us towards self-actualisation and ever deeper levels of consciousness.

The Discipline of Learning – A spiritual practice

The discipline of completing the learning cycle through a review or by journaling can help us to draw insights and lessons from current and past experiences and enhance the additional challenge of applying those lessons in the future. The expression or communication of our thoughts and feelings is a vital part of the learning process. It helps clarify and make sense of what we have, or what we're experiencing. I have included a format for keeping a journal at Annex B, and I recommend this as a regular practice - in your 4th Space - again, bringing a discipline into this spiritual quest.

The Outer Journey

Before we set out on our journey, we first need to know more about where we are travelling and why. Unless we have a clear sense of why it is important to follow this challenging path and master the desires of our own animal nature, we do not stand a chance of breaking the chains which hold us. There are some more important questions to answer to bring this clarity. So, here, I begin to explore the mystery of life and of our lives.

THE MEANING AND PURPOSE OF LIFE

Who am I? Why am I here - is there a purpose to life or am I just a temporary gathering of dust? And, if there is a purpose, how should I live my life to fulfil it? Those questions have circled around us since we came out of the trees. Our search for meaning has led us to the forming of great religions, the building of great temples, the writing of so many sacred texts, the development of spiritual practices and codes of behaviour. Seeking this deeper purpose to life is at the heart of the spiritual life.

The Native Americans talk of the purpose of life as the education of the soul. This is my understanding too, based on sacred writings, teachings, observations and personal experience. I do not understand the origins of this purpose but I see an interconnection between all life, between all things in existence. I also understand that the education and evolution of each individual element, each soul, leads to the evolution of the whole: expanding the universal consciousness. I have included here some notes from my mystical school and my teacher William Lambert. They have influenced greatly my own philosophy.

We are like a diver at the bottom of the sea; we have travelled a long, long way from our true source and home. Yet, at the same time, we are closer to that Mother Ship to the source than the thickness of our skin; closer than a breath away. Our Atman or True Self has been sent forth from the source of all things, has come through many regions, through the Idea of Man and has been given a Spiritual Plan which has projected itself into the Soul Body. The soul is like a reflection of the personality; the spirit is the character.

These levels of information reflect themselves into the different colours of the aura. The aura changes from life to life according to the new plan and it can even change within our lifetime as we pass through different experiences. Our soul and spirit and eternal light of the True Self come into the temple of our physical body. The seed of light joins our physical body at the moment of conception – the sperm, the egg and the seed of light. It builds the body, passing through every stage of evolution in the nine months. That life force remains in the heart chakra and is the sum of every life you have ever lived. In different lifetimes, we have been both man and woman, rich and poor, in order that our consciousness might be refined. We are all part of the refinement of the whole of human consciousness for we are part of that great ocean. We are, in a way, like bubbles in the sea and, ultimately, after thousands of years and many lives, when we have purified our consciousness, we shall be allowed to merge back into the ocean itself. We shall become part of the universal consciousness.

Yet always, if there is a special task for us to do we shall be able to return to help mankind. An example of this is the great Avatars and teachers, such as Jesus, Buddha, Sai Baba and others. They come with the great mission of improving the flow

*of the tide and to put mankind back onto the path into the light.
We all need to listen more to our higher mind, higher ego and
more experienced consciousness. We need to regularly meditate
in order to listen to the voice of God speaking to us.*

*Our physical self has evolved over millions and millions of
years, during which time the consciousness of the physical body
has passed through many levels. We have come through different
routes and we have affinities going back to particular things. So,
some people have green fingers and may become florists or
horticulturists, while others may have an affinity with animals
and become farmers. Some may have an affinity with the Earth
itself and become miners or geologists. Others may have an
affinity with the sea and love to swim or fish or sail the oceans. So,
we are a continuation of Earth and heaven. Sometimes we listen to
our Earth consciousness and our body and its demands, its
desires, its wishes and needs, and at other times we are more
attuned to our own invisible self. We know a great deal but have
forgotten much. We can reawaken much of this by our meditation,
self-discipline, duty and devotion to the higher needs.*

Make it Your Own

There are many other teachings, and the challenge for the mystic is
to find their own way to explore and express the spiritual impulse
without the politics and trauma that seem, invariably, to come with
formal religion, to find ways to lift us out of our animal, instinctive
nature and take us on a path to higher levels of consciousness.

At each stage of this journey, capture in your own words your
understanding and your commitments. Even if you already follow a
religion, capture your understanding of the beliefs, principles and
practices in your own words. It will push you to go deeper into the
essence of that tradition rather than simply accept the symbols, the
mantras and the rituals without taking personal responsibility for
the path you have chosen.

WALKING ON THE MOUNTAIN

I love the idea of walking the mountain as a metaphor for our spiritual life. The sense of moving upwards towards the heavens, to the peaks where we will see clearly all that is. The idea of the challenges that we face as we climb or the desire just to rest and enjoy the place we are in now. The understanding that grows as we move around the mountain and see that each place will see a different perspective of those peaks and identify different paths to take us there.

Yet, like the hero's journey, we need to understand fully the metaphor. The journey on the mountain also represents our inner journey as we seek the gold deep within us. Remember:

Mysticism is primarily an inner journey, and the path that this journey follows is the experience of your own life, wherever you are and whoever you are with.

The Paths on the Mountain

Although I am seeking a way that breaks with the deeply embedded forces of society and of our own nature, I know that the secrets of the mountain are held in the multitude of spiritual traditions. We can study and learn from those maps.

So, let's explore. I was brought up as a Christian and even went to a Methodist school. I have recited the Creed and celebrated the birth, the life and the resurrection of Jesus. I have even visited the stable in Bethlehem and walked the Via Dolorosa in Jerusalem. Yet it has been through other traditions that I have felt my soul sing. I studied other religions at school and as part of my mystical training on my university programme of Spiritual Development and Facilitation

34

Seeking Inspiration

I have brought together just one or two elements from some of those maps to stimulate and inspire your own thoughts. There is no logical order or attempt to make it a comprehensive list. Nor have I attempted to summarise or describe any of them fully here. There are many books on these great religions and you can also explore them on the internet to give you a feel for their philosophy and principles. Spend some time exploring these different perspectives of the mountain – the monotheistic traditions, the Eastern philosophies and indigenous traditions – not to follow them, but to learn from them.

Before you begin reading, I would like to introduce you to a spiritual practice I have found to be very powerful and a way to tune into your intuition. It is called Lecto Divina.

Lecto Divina – listen to the quiet voice of the soul

In the Christian tradition, the art of *Lecto Divina* begins with cultivating the ability to listen deeply, to hear 'with the ear of our hearts.' It is a practice for followers to read the bible or sacred texts to gain a deeper personal connection through the words. It can be used as a mindfulness practice for any text which may hold a special meaning for you; practise it as you explore these other traditions.

As you read, listen through your feelings and, if you find a passage or an idea which resonates in some way, then sit with it. Notice if it raises up any images or deep memories, let it interact with your thoughts, your fears and your dreams. Keep a note of the elements that resonate strongly with you – not just at the intellectual level. You are listening for the quiet voice of your soul.

Choosing Our Path

We are most likely to be drawn into a religion through our parents, our schooling or local culture. We can also be influenced in how we express our spiritual impulse by our personality. Some will enjoy the search for truth, others will seek expression through their work. The extroverts may seek communities to belong to while the introverts may seek solitude and quiet reflection. Some will seek unity and harmony within themselves and in the world and some will seek to devote their lives to a great vision or the highest values. The beauty of choosing your own path is that you find what is meaningful and impactful for you, so do not feel constrained. What I would say, though, is that the gateway to learning and evolving is often the area we feel least comfortable in. So, as well as choosing spiritual practices which feel right, be prepared to experiment with those that don't.

All Different, All Unique

We are all a unique blend of characteristics. Do not feel constrained by any of them, just be aware of them. Let me give you an example. I am a strong introvert, and yet I have found that the gateway to expressing my own impulse has been through action and service as well as the times of solitude. Be prepared to step outside the 'comfort zone' of your preferences and explore other dimensions of yourself.

Maps for the Mystic

In my own Western culture, spiritual development has been dominated by the great monotheistic traditions. Even within these, though, there are different sects and branches. In this new Aquarian Age, there have been many new spiritual practices and a revival of many ancient ones. There are thought to be some 4,300 different religions in the world now. So, there is an incredible range of different spiritual maps to help us choose our own path. Which is the right path? How will I choose? Can I betray my parents? Will I anger the gods of my childhood or my family, or their representatives if I walk a different path? It is easy for me to give an answer.

My parents always encouraged me to follow my own path, even when it was risky and rocky. I was never indoctrinated in a religion or a cult and have always been able to choose for myself. Throughout history – and in many parts of the world today, people have killed and been killed for making the kind of choice that I am suggesting here. We need to consider our personal circumstances and physical safety, but balance that with the importance of living our own lives – not someone else's.

Here, I have just included elements from the maps that have inspired me.

THE FIVE LEVELS OF ATTACHMENT

I shall start with a piece drawn from the writings of Don Miguel Ruiz about the Toltec tradition. When we first moved from hunting and gathering to farming the land, we no longer lived in harmony with nature and the land; we started to own it and saw it as something to exploit. That drive to accumulate wealth and power has spread to all parts of our life and our world. *The five levels of attachment* brings an awareness, an understanding of these inner drives.

Critical for Our Future

The need to develop non-attachment and detachment are themes across traditions. You will see it in the Tao Te Ching below, and it is a core principle of the Buddhist Four Noble Truths. I start with it because, for me, it is a critical requirement for individual development, and even more so for change in our societies. Attachment to our ideas prevents creativity; attachment to beliefs leads to bigotry and violence. Do not underestimate the power of attachment to disrupt even the best of intentions: within others as they seek to impose their views on you; within yourself as you fight back to defend your own path. To develop openness and acceptance requires great awareness and self-control.

The Levels of Attachment

The first level of attachment represents the **Authentic Self**, the living being that is the full potential of life. It describes that force that not only animates the body but also gives life to our mind and soul. The Creative Source, the seed of light or Atman.

At the second level of attachment, **Preference**, we still move with the awareness of the authentic self. We recognise our ability to attach ourselves to something as we engage in the present moment, but we are also able to let go of the attachment when the moment has passed.

The third level of attachment is **Identity**. You take your knowledge with you and begin to shape parts of your life around this identity; your attachment bleeds into a world that has nothing to do with it.

The fourth level of attachment, **Internalisation**, describes a degree of attachment to knowledge where our identity becomes the model by which we accept ourselves. This is domestication through attachment.

The fifth level of attachment is **Fanaticism**. Whenever we believe something without question, we are at risk for attachment at this most extreme level - it can exist in the most unlikely places.

An Example of Levels of Attachment

Don Miguel explains it wonderfully in a simple example of how it might impact on our love of football. At level one, we just love the game and enjoy it wherever we see it. At level two, we begin to develop a preference for the outcome of a game; I prefer it when Leicester beat Liverpool but, at the end of the game, win or lose, I move on to the next game. At level 3, our support for the team begins to shape our identity, the people we mix with and our view of others. I wear the colours. At level 4, I now feel the outcome of the game - win and I am in a great place, I feel good about myself; lose and I feel a sense of anger - and I may well take out that anger on the followers of the opposing team. You can see how this easily moves then to the fanatical devotion of level 5 where I will sacrifice my own life or take that of another in service to my belief or my cause. And you can see how these levels can be seen in the religions of the world - and used by those in power to commit acts of violence. No religion is exempt - from the crusades and the Spanish Inquisition to the extremists of Islam and Buddhism today.

My Lesson – Guard Against Attachment

Attachment, nature or nurture? Invariably, when that question is asked, the answer is 'Yes'. It will be a mix of both. I know for certain that the drive is a part of my character and I feel strong attachments, for example, to my family, to my friends, to my country, to my old regiment and to my old school. I have become more conscious of them through my mindfulness practice and the growing awareness of our unconscious biases. It is a part of my spiritual journey to guard against the effects of strong attachment and to stay open to new understanding, new ideas and new people.

MY LAW – TIEME RANAPIRI

I became acquainted with some elements of the Maori tradition, the indigenous people of New Zealand, when I read the wonderful book *Legacy* by James Kerr. One of the best books on leadership I have read, it describes many of the principles which underpin the incredible sporting success of the All Blacks, the New Zealand national rugby team. They draw much from the Maori heritage.

'My Law' is a poem written by a Maori. I love it because it captures, in such a simple and beautiful way, so much of the traditions of Theosophy, spiritual psychotherapy, the Vedic traditions and the teachings of the Buddha. More than any other script I have come across, it simply and effectively captures a whole philosophy of life and the meaning of life.

> The sun may be clouded, yet ever the sun
> Will sweep on its course till the Cycle is run
> And when into chaos the system is hurled
> Again, shall the Builder reshape a new world
>
> Your path may be clouded, uncertain your goal:
> Move on – for your orbit is fixed to your soul.
> And though it may lead into darkness of night
> The torch of the Builder shall give it new light

You were. You will be! Know this while you are:
Your spirit has travelled both long and afar.
It came from the Source, to the Source it returns -
The Spark which was lighted eternally burns.

It slept in a jewel. It leapt in a wave.
It roamed in the forest. It rose from the grave.
It took on strange garbs for long eons of years
And now in the soul of yourself it appears.

From body to body your spirit speeds on
It seeks a new form when the old one has gone
And the form that it finds is the fabric you wrought
On the loom of the Mind from the fibre of Thought.
As dew is drawn upwards, in rain to descend
Your thoughts drift away and in Destiny blend.
You cannot escape them, for petty or great,
Or evil or noble, they fashion your Fate

Somewhere on some planet, sometime and somehow
Your life will reflect your thoughts of your Now.
My Law is unerring, no blood can atone -
The structure you built you will live in – alone.
From cycle to cycle, through time and through space
Your lives with your longings will ever keep pace
And all that you ask for, and all you desire
Must come at your bidding, as flame out of fire.

Once list' to that Voice and all tumult is done -
Your life is the Life of the Infinite one.
In the hurrying race, you are conscious of pause
With love for the purpose, and love for the Cause.

You are your own Devil, you are your own God
You fashioned the paths your footsteps have trod.
And no one can save you from Error or Sin
Until you have hark'd to the Spirit within.

Attributed to a Maori, Tieme Ranapiri

My Lessons

The poem captures certain important principles for me. The cyclic
evolution of the cosmos and the long path of soul evolution from
the lowest kingdom of nature up to the human kingdom and
eventually beyond. It describes the ongoing process of reincarnation and the influence of our own thoughts and consciousness
upon our future (the idea of karma). It describes the oneness and
divine nature of all life and, most important in relation to this
journal, the law of self-created destiny, which makes each of us
solely responsible for our own actions.

SPIRITUAL PSYCHOTHERAPY

Spiritual Psychotherapy contains the teachings and practices that
underpinned my own mystical school. It has had a profound impact
on my own path. I have to admit to not much liking the name
'spiritual psychotherapy' but the philosophy itself, I did. The 'school'
combines natural healing processes, particularly light, colour and
sound, with spiritual science and wisdom that has been passed
down through the centuries. It is based on the work and teachings
of Ronald Beesley, a mystic and healer who established the College
of Psychotherapeutics in 1952.

It encourages discerment, personal responsibility for our health,
and provides practical guidance for living in the world. It also

stretches the boundaries of the mind, challenging our thinking, our concentration and our will with a comprehensive philosophy that touches the essence of all faiths. It also works at the soul level, awakening a deeper and deeper understanding of our place in the cosmos, our purpose in life and the support available to us on our spiritual journey. It is truly a mystical school.

The Principles

The main principles of the philosophy are:

Unity – all is mind, but on many different levels and manifesting in many different forms. Awareness of this oneness, of this sense of purpose helps change our perspective and our approach to our life and to life around us.

Light – light and dark weave their magical dance and create all that is. It is Ying and Yang, it is the duality or our world. It is the many levels of manifesting energy: form, colour and sound.

Love – this is the binding force of the cosmos manifesting in more and more subtle levels up to the expression of pure unconditional love.

Creation and Evolution – this is the divine plan in action. Each element, formed of light and love, evolving in accordance with their destiny, within the divine plan.

Order (Law) and Peace – this is the plan working out perfectly in the rhythm of the cosmos. Spirals within spirals in a great cycle of chaos and order, creation and destruction, birth and re-birth. This is the natural order of the cosmos and includes the 'iron' law of cause and effect.

My Lessons

There are many lessons that I have taken from spiritual psycho-therapy. The healing practices, the use of sound and colour to deal with the symptoms of disease and restore health. Perhaps more important, though, has been to apply the principles and practices to deal with the underying cause and create the living conditions for mind, body and soul that prevent these imbalances and problems from occurring.

TAO TE CHING

I began to read the Tao Te Ching when I started to practise Tai Chi Chuan on leaving the army. I was looking for a physical exercise that wasn't going to be too damaging to my knees, but didn't want to practise the 'hard' martial arts - I reckoned I'd had enough of that in my army days. It was a great bonus to find that there is such an incredible philosophy lying behind the physical form. I have drawn much inspiration from Lao Tzu's words over the years.

There is no logical flow to the Tao Te Ching and this seems to fit with the story of how Lao Tzu had to be persuaded to write down his thinking. It reads like the remembering of an old sage, struggling to capture the wonder of his wisdom and the mystery of the indescribable. There are repetitions that give the sense of concern to get some of the more important messages across – while acknowledging that . . .

My words are easy to understand and easy to perform

Yet no man under heaven knows them or
practices them

Verse 70

There is a great deal written on detachment and yet there is a feeling that Lao Tzu, while being close, could not lose his exasperation, frustration and despair at the impact of desire and fear in the world he was walking away from. I find that reassuring - that even the great, evolved souls find it challenging to live in this world and feel the whole range of emotions.

There is a mix both of wisdom and practical guidelines as to how to live. I have captured just a few of his verses here and summarised what I have drawn from his work. I hope it inspires you to read a full translation.

The Tao

The Nature of Life
His words describing the Tao can give us an understanding of the nature of the cosmos, God, the universal consciousness or some other expression which seeks to capture 'all that is'. Lao Tzu comes back to the definition of the Tao through his 81 verses:

The Tao that can be told is not the eternal Tao

Verse 1

Look it cannot be seen – it is beyond form …
Stand before it and there is no beginning
Follow it and there is no end.

Verse 14

He strives to describe it but also to stress the importance of remembering it – staying grounded in it. To me, it suggests the importance of staying connected to our spiritual impulse and not getting seduced by our instinctive nature, the lure of the senses and desire for material 'wealth'.

> *Keeping to the main road is easy,*
> *But people love to be side-tracked.*
>
> Verse 53

That is also a great reminder to me, of how easy it is to know all the right things that I should be doing – but, maybe, I will start tomorrow, or perhaps I will do my meditation when I have finished watching this programme, after I have made that call ... when I am in a better mood ...

Detachment

I mentioned this earlier as a common theme in religions like Buddhism and the pure Christian faith. It links closely to the idea of non-attachment but it is of a higher order. It allows you to be at one with the Tao. This mastery of desire and selflessness is the primal virtue.

> *The sage stays behind, thus he is ahead.*
> *He is detached, thus at one with all.*
> *Through selfless action, he attains fulfilment.*
>
> Verse 7

Non-Attachment and Desire

The ability to break free from the constraints of desire is central to the Tao Te Ching. I counted 11 verses where it was referred to and many more where it is alluded to. To Lao Tzu, mastering our desire is the key – and yet, in his way he acknowledges that in attempting to master it, in desiring mastery, we lose the fight. There is one of the ambiguities that I mentioned before.

46

There is no greater sin than desire

No greater curse than discontent
No greater misfortune than wanting something for yourself
Therefore, he who knows that enough is enough will always
have enough.

Verse 46

He who is attached to things will suffer much.
He who saves will suffer heavy loss.
A contented man is never disappointed.

Verse 44

Freedom or Emptiness
Much of the Tao Te Ching is encouraging 'letting go' of 'becoming empty' and attaining the freedom from the constraints of desire and ambition.

Therefore, the sage seeks freedom from desire
He does not collect precious things
He learns not to hold onto ideas.

Verse 64

Centredness, Balance, Calmness and Constancy

Hold fast to the centre.

Verse 5

Better stop short than fill to the brim
Over sharpen the blade, and the edge will blunt.

Verse 9

Knowing constancy is insight.
Not knowing constancy leads to disaster.

Verse 16

In nine verses, Lao Tzu refers to the need for balance and staying centred. This does not mean that you withdraw or deny aspects of the world or yourself; it is developing the ability to 'be in the world but not of it', to be able to experience the full range of emotions but to be able to control your response, to see them for what they are. The Buddhists will talk of equanimity and the middle way; this is the same idea. We know that life is constantly changing, that we will experience both success and failure, love and loss, joy and sadness. Staying centred means that we smile but not too broadly, we cry but not too loudly, we celebrate our success but stay humble and considerate of others. When we lose, we feel the anger and pain but acknowledge the victor and look to learn from the loss. You might see the foundations of sportsmanship in there.

> *Therefore, the sage travelling all day*
> *Does not lose sight of his baggage*
> *Though there are beautiful things to be seen*
> *He remains unattached and calm.*
>
> Verse 26

Verse 28 captures the paradox that Lao Tzu encourages us to live. The symbol of Tai Chi represents this dialectic approach:

> *Know the strength of man*
> *But keep a woman's care ...*
> *Know the white,*
> *But keep the black!*
> *Be an example to the world ...*
> *Know honour*
>
> *Yet keep humility*

Simplicity and Childlikeness

Remember when I talked about the hero's journey? I mentioned how we were born in a pure state, connected to the great consciousness. Becoming or being like the child is a theme that Lao Tzu uses throughout the verses. He warns against the dangers of the intellect and our ability to confuse and cloud things with our desire.

> *The sage has no mind of his own ...*
> *The sage is shy and humble – to the world he seems confusing ...*
> *He behaves like a little child.*
>
> Verse 49

> *When wisdom and intelligence are born,*
> *The great pretence begins.*
>
> Verse 18

He encourages us to follow our true nature, to seek the gold that lies beneath, and not be distracted by desire.

> *It is more important*
> *To see the simplicity*
> *To realise one's true nature*
> *And temper desire*
>
> Verse 19

Developing Resilience

You might be glad to know that he acknowledges the difficulty of following this path in the world. He talks in many places of being misunderstood by others and of the loneliness and doubt that can accompany this Tao. I did warn you that the path of the mystic is a lonely one!

Other men are sharp and clever,
But I alone am dull and stupid ...
But I alone am aimless and depressed.
I am different.
I am nourished by the great mother.

Verse 20

So, he highlights the importance of developing resilience and perseverance.

Mastering others requires force:
Mastering the self needs strength
He who knows he has enough is rich
Perseverance is a sign of will power.

Verse 33

A Sense of Rightness and Non-Action

One of the great traditions that I feel drawn to is what is now known as the Kemetic tradition of Ancient Egypt. They had no word for religion as, to them, everything was spirit; it was indivisible from daily life and existence. In particular, I love the idea of Ma'at.

The Rule of Ma'at was the guiding force behind the governance of this incredible civilisation and represented the Goddess Ma'at. Ma'at was paired with Thoth, who represented truth. In their wisdom, the Egyptians recognised that the concept of truth represented by Thoth was too hard, too absolute to deal with the intricacies and nuances of life, Ma'at was more a sense of rightness, of balance which, if maintained, would lead to harmony.

Lao Tzu acknowledges this lack of absolute knowledge and truth, that there are some questions that we just don't know the answer to. How we can judge what is better or worse if the Tao is everything. There are times when we just go with our inner guidance:

Therefore, the sage is guided by what he feels and not
by what he sees.
He lets go of this and chooses that.

Verse 12

And then Lao Tzu offers guidance as to what these virtues are throughout the Tao Te Ching. In Verse 8 he talks of truth, justice and kindness. In Verse 67 he talks of his three treasures: mercy, economy and of 'daring not to be ahead of others'. Always there is the practice of 'flowing with' rather than struggling against, and he stresses, in many verses, the importance of this 'non-action'.

Yield and overcome
Bend and be straight ...
Not putting on a display
They shine forth ...
They do not quarrel
So, no one quarrels with them.

Verse 21

Lessons for Me

You can see the themes emerging. The idea of 'living in hamony with' rather than seeking to impose our will. The Tai Chi Chuan martial art is based on that principle. The idea of staying centred and developing detachment; this is the principle underpinning my 4th Space practice. I have often quoted Lao Tzu on my leadership programmes; he was advocating the idea of empowerment some 2500 years ago.

THE EIGHTFOLD PATH

There is much more to Buddhism than the Eightfold Path and I do recommend that you explore the principles underpinning this religion or philosophy. I think that much of the essence is captured in the Maori poem, 'My Way', above. It is one of the great paths on this mountain. I particularly like the Eightfold Path because, regardless of whether you are a Buddhist or not, it provides wonderful guidance as to how to navigate the mountain. It describes eight aspects of life to be integrated into our everyday living. It is not a 'commandment', rather it is a guidance to reflect on and then adopt when you are ready to commit to following this path. Buddhism doesn't ask for blind faith; it seeks to promote learning and a process of self-discovery. That is another reason I love so much of this philosophy.

The meaning of 'right' has several aspects, and includes an ethical and a balanced, or middle, way. It is as much a feeling or intuition; 'a sense of rightness' which we feel inside when we have made the right choice. Again, you can see the similarity with the Law of Ma'at in Ancient Egypt.

Right Understanding or Right View

This is a vital step on the path. To see life, the world and everything in it as it is, not as we believe it to be or want it to be. We can study books, we can listen to great teachers or the opinions of others and they might help add to our knowledge. At a deeper level, though, it is direct personal experience that will lead us to Right Understanding. The Buddha said, 'My teaching is a method to experience reality and not reality itself, just as **a finger pointing at the moon is not the moon itself.** A thinking person makes use of the finger to see the moon. A person who only looks at the finger and mistakes it for the moon will never see the real moon.'

Right Intention

The second step on the Eightfold Path is Right Intent. This is a commitment to follow the upward path, to climb the mountain. Right Understanding shows us the nature of life, the resources we have and the challenges we face. Right Intent to follow this path unerringly comes from the heart, from the centre of love. It involves recognising the oneness of all life and compassion for all that life, beginning with yourself. The mountain we climb here is our journey through life.

With Right Intent and Right Understanding, we can then seek to remove desire, the cause of the suffering defined in the Four Noble Truths.

Right Speech

Right Speech is the next step on the path. When I was a child, when my sister teased me, I was told, 'Remember, sticks and stones may break my bones, but words can never hurt me.' It didn't seem to work that way. The power of the spoken word - to inspire, to humiliate, to encourage, to wound - is immense. How often have I regretted words spoken or written in haste? Each of us has experienced that power.

Right speech involves speaking our truth, at the same time being aware of the impact of our words, of idle gossip and of repeating rumours. Communicating thoughtfully helps to unite others, and can heal dissention. By resolving never to speak unkindly, or in anger, a spirit of consideration evolves which moves us closer to everyday compassionate living.

Right Action

Right Action involves us approaching life with consideration for others and for the world we live in. It includes the honouring of agreements and promises we make both in our private and business lives. Right Action also encompasses the five precepts which were given by the Buddha; not to kill, steal, lie, to avoid sexual misconduct and not to take drugs or other intoxicants. It includes our relationship with the environment and with all forms of life, acting with a view to future generations.

Right Livelihood

Following on from Right Action comes Right Livelihood. If our work does not respect all life, then it will be a barrier to progress on the spiritual path. Buddhism promotes the principle of equality of all living beings and respect for all life. It discourages dealing in harmful drugs and intoxicants, weapons and harm to animal or human life. This includes all forms of slavery or abuse.

Finally, Right Livelihood encourages us to undertake work, paid or voluntary, which serves others and supports the community.

Right Effort

Right Effort means cultivating an enthusiasm, a positive attitude and sense of purpose – all in a balanced way. When I play a golf or cricket shot, if I try to hit it the ball too hard, it tends to go wrong. That's not quite true, it always goes wrong. So, not too tense, not too relaxed – Right Effort brings a balanced, steady and cheerful sense of determination. In nurturing this attitude, again there is need for balance. We should embrace an honest assessment of our performance but leave the negative self-talk, the negative emotions of jealousy, anger or hatred behind us. Right Effort equates to positive thinking, followed by focused action.

Right Mindfulness

Right Mindfulness means being fully present, fully aware of all that is going on inside us and outside us, in that moment – with a sense of curiosity and without judgement. Our mind is like 'a hundred chattering monkeys on the branch of a tree' – taking our attention to the past, to the future, to noises and sights around us. We spend little time being fully present, now.

Right Mindfulness is the discipline to bring our attention fully into the present. It is closely linked with meditation and can be a stepping stone to meditation. By developing this practice, we develop self-awareness, seeing how old patterns and habits, fears and prejudices impact on us. We develop a sense of curiosity and openness, a focus and emotional regulation and empathy and an attunement with the world and people around us.

Right Concentration

Once the mind is uncluttered and disciplined, we can focus it where we choose. Right Concentration involves turning the mind to focus on an object, such as a flower, or a candle, or a concept such as loving compassion. This forms the next part of the meditation process. Right Concentration implies that we select worthy directions for the concentration of the mind. Again, the sense of rightness in all that we do.

The benefits of Right Mindfulness and Right Concentration are significant as they teach the mind to see things not as we are programmed to seeing them, but as they really are. At the same time, they also lead to a feeling of calm and peace with the world. By being in the moment and being able to concentrate effectively, a sense of joy in the moment is felt. Release from the control of past pains and future mind games takes us closer to freedom from suffering.

Lessons for Me

What I take from the Eightfold Path is the importance of looking at the whole picture, the whole of life. Words and actions are important but they are the 'end result' of our underlying awareness and understanding, of the quality of our thinking, of our attitudes and approach to life.

Other Religions

There are some 4300 religions in our modern world. There is so much to learn from their teachings and so much to gain from some of their practices if we can look beyond the rules and rituals. As with all things, there is a good side and a shadow side. There is much to explore and many different perspectives of the mountain and its nature.

YOUR PATH

Spend time gathering your own thoughts and reflections on the nature of this life, of all life. Listen to your own intuition as you gather knowledge from the great traditions. Capture your sense of purpose. There is a space at the end of the journal to capture your thoughts but there is no deadline – it is not an exam. It is just the beginning of the journey of discovery.

Here is an example of how I have tried to use poetry to capture my own thoughts at one stage on my journey.

Why?
(Peter Danby 2019)

Travelling the world, seeing the incredible technological advances and the privileged lives of the wealthy (and I include myself in that group). Travelling the world, seeing the depths of poverty, of violence and abuse. How often do I ask the question, 'Why?' Is there any meaning or purpose to what seems to be the lottery of life? My own understanding, drawn from my teachings, my studies and my own life experiences is 'Yes, there is.' I should perhaps explain the opening words of the poem are from the Vedic traditions; Atman, the seed of light, or what we might call the soul of each person and Brahman, the universal 'force' the source of all that is and all that will be. What some might call God.

Atman in Brahman, Brahman in Atman
We are all a part of the whole
And we live each life in its service
And to further develop our soul.

That soul has lived many lives
And every life that we that chose
Was linked to both those great missions;
As, from the darkness, we rose.

So, you see, the suffering of others
And the lives that are filled full of pain
Are not without meaning or purpose
Each life is lived for our gain.

The lessons, if we can just see them,
Are lessons of anger and hate,
But also of love and compassion
And the patience to struggle or wait.

So, the beggar who lies in the doorway
Or the refugees on the beach
Might just be great souls, who have chosen
To come back in this life to teach.

So, look once again at your life
And see it and the world in this light,
As a world that is meant for our learning
And not just a hell where we fight.

And as, through our lives, we awaken
And feel our consciousness shift
The veils of darkness will open
And we will see every life as a gift.

So, yes, each life has a purpose,
We are all a part of the whole
And each life is lived in its service
And to further develop the soul.

Your View of the Mountain ... Will Change as You Walk

You may be thinking, 'Who am I to write about the meaning of life?' The answer is that we will always write from our current level of understanding - from where we stand on the mountain. The important things are first, that it is your understanding and, second, that you are open to new insights as you walk higher on this path.

Let me give you one example of how my own understanding has shifted. When I first started out on my spiritual journey, I was challenged by one of the sayings attributed to Jesus.

'Give up all and follow me.'

58

I was happily married with two wonderful children, and could not see how I could even begin to 'give up all'. I asked for guidance and, remembering the advice of my teacher at the time to ask to be guided to the right books and the right people, I picked a book at random from his library. I opened the book and on that very page was a description of the meaning of sacrifice – of giving something up for something greater. The author went on to say that there could be no greater love than the unconditional love of a mother or father for their children of a husband for his wife, and would a loving God demand you to give up those you love? Co-incidence?

The story doesn't end there. I have enjoyed exploring many traditions over the years and there is one theme which seems to keep appearing: the idea of detachment, of mastering desire, of emptiness and accepting ourselves and our situation without expectation or desire. In other words, the idea of 'giving up all desire for material wealth and sensual pleasures and following . . . a path to higher consciousness.' There it is again, 'Give up all and follow me.' Now, it makes much more sense. Personal development can be a slow unfolding rather than a rapid rise and it has taken me many years. Perhaps I could have gone faster but, then again, I may have missed something if I had.

Preparing the Vehicle

So, we have looked the terrain and studied the maps ready for the outer journey. Before we go on to set the direction and decide how we will travel, we need to understand as much as we can about the vehicle we are travelling in, the nature of self. The inner journey and the timeless challenge of personal mastery.

The Inner Journey

THE TIMELESS CHALLENGE
OF PERSONAL MASTERY

Describing the path that we want to take and the moral code we choose to live by is easy. The real challenge is to keep following that path when the going gets tough, when we encounter the reality of the outside world. When your vehicle, your self, seems to have a mind of its own, getting pulled this way and that by forces you do not understand.

It has always been that way, as Lao Tzu reminds us.

My words are easy to understand and easy to perform
Yet no man under heaven knows them or practices them.

Verse 70

St Augustine also reminds us how easy it is to forget the inner journey as we walk through life.

People travel to wonder
At the height of mountains
At the huge waves of the sea
At the long courses of the rivers, at the vast compass of the ocean
At the circular motion of the stars
And pass themselves by without wondering.

St Augustine

Finally, from Mohatmas Gandhi.

To put the world in order, we must first put the nation in order; to put the nation in order, we must first put the family in order; to put the family in order; we must first cultivate our personal life; we must first set our hearts right.

This seems to be particularly relevant today as we struggle to deal with the impact of our behaviours on our planet. We look to the political leaders, to the business leaders, and yet, how many of us are prepared to take responsibility for our own way of life, for making the changes that we demand of others, in Gandhi's famous words, to *'be the change you wish to see in the world'*?

Know Thy Self

How much do we know about this body, this mind, this self that we inhabit now? Just what is our 'potential'? What physical, mental and psychic talents do we have and how can we use them more effectively? What do we know about our instinct and emotions and how can learn to master them - using them with skill rather than them controlling us?

In my work, the development of leadership in people of all ages, one definition of leadership is, 'being yourself more, with skill.' This is a theme in many leadership studies today; we hear expressions like, 'be your best self.' 'bring your whole self to work' or 'be authentic.' It all sounds so simple, so easy to say, and yet far from easy to do. First we need to understand the self and all that it involves and then, harder still, we can set about mastering and developing it. Here is what I wrote as I was creating the Inspire: Sport & Leadership programme for my charity.

INSPIRE

The Background

The greatest challenge that we continue to face as humans is not the change in the world around us, however fast. Nor is to continue to grow our intellect, develop new scientific knowledge, grow our economies or achieve higher standards in our schools and universities. The greatest challenge that we face is to master our own instinctive nature, the nature that instantaneously judges and condemns, prompts us to fight or fly, justifies and rationalises any decision or behaviour which fits our own needs or those closest to us. The conscious and unconscious abuse of power – in relationships, in families, in communities, in every form of social, sporting, academic or political organisation – has remained the greatest shaping force in the world of people throughout history – and remains so today.

Our education not only fails to address or help in this challenge, it will often reinforce or exacerbate it. Rather than being taught discernment, children are taught beliefs. Rather than learning awareness, understanding and self-discipline, they are taught to be obedient. They are taught to hate other ethnic, national or religious groups from the cradle by parents, by teachers and by their community. Even in the 'developed' countries, politicians and priests still seek and gain power by appealing to these self-centred, instinctive needs. And, they learn to resolve conflict through violence and to use power to inflict pain, suffering and death.

The education of our children has to change if we are to break this endless cycle of mistrust, hatred, violence – mistrust, hatred, violence. Changing our nature may be possible, it may not, but we can, through education, raise awareness and understanding and develop the ability to choose different responses within relationships and between groups, tribes and countries. Through this process we can enable those other dimensions of our nature to play a more dominant role in our world; compassion, empathy, humility and love.

It is hard enough to change one person, just yourself. To change the world will require people in positions of power to support a process which, ultimately, will lead to a change in how that power is perceived and used. They need to be prepared to give up their power, to defy their own instinctive nature and hold their own beliefs lightly. Difficult certainly. Impossible, maybe. The alternative is not to make the attempt – and live with the abuse, live with the corruption, live with the slaughter. That seems to me to be an easy choice to make – but then, I am not in that position of power.

This quest for mastery has been our greatest challenge since the dawn of humanity. And, despite advances in many fields of human endeavour and the incredible changes that we face in the immediate future, it remains our greatest challenge today. So, who are we? What is this self?

THE NATURE OF THE HUMAN ANIMAL

In his book *The Chimp Paradox*, the sports psychologist Dr Stephen Peters, creates a simple three-part model to explain our incredibly complex brain and how different parts fight for control of our behaviour. Seeing ourselves as slightly more evolved animals rather than superior beings is an important step on our journey. It helps us to see the challenge we face.

The Chimp, the Human and the Computer

The first element of Peters' model describes 'the chimp', or our emotional and instinctive nature. This represents the most ancient part of our brain, designed to enable us to survive in a world full of predators and threats, of hierarchies and fundamental physiological needs. The second he describes as the human, which is the seat of our logic and of our social conscience. These two 'characters' compete for control of our words and actions although, as Peters describes it, the chimp is five times stronger and faster than the human.

> *A grandfather was explaining to his grandson that within him and within each of us there are two tigers fighting for control. One represents all that is negative about us: anger, hatred, greed, jealousy and the like. The other represents all that is virtuous about us; love, joy, compassion, generosity and so forth.*
>
> *The young boy thought for a while and then asked, 'So which one will win within me. Grandfather?'*
>
> *'That is easy,' he said. 'The one that you feed.'*
>
> Old Chinese Story

The third element in the model he calls 'the computer', and it is programmed with our experiences, personal belief patterns and cultural norms. It holds all of our 'scripts', our memories and the stories about our self, about others and our life, and it feeds the chimp and the human with the information that they need to react to all the situations we face as we go through life.

Our Instinctive Nature

It scares me just how much of our life is directed by this part of our nature, this part of our brain. When you see that our genetic make-up is approximately 99% the same as chimpanzees, 80% the same as cows then it makes sense – but it's still scary. Partly because we like to think of ourselves as intelligent, rational and superior beings.

We are hard wired to survive and to safeguard our genetic inheritance. The basic human needs and drives that the psychologists have identified over the years are closely linked to that drive; hunger, sex, safety – including belonging to a family, troop or gang. We are able, in a glance, to identify a threat – from a sound, from a facial expression – and instantly make a judgement. That speed of reaction, in our modern world, enables us to drive cars at high speed or play a tennis ball being fired at us at 120 mph. It also, consciously or unconsciously, enables us to make judgements about people – based on physical appearance and the stories that we hold in our 'computer'. These are our prejudices and biases and, together with our need for status and power, they have shaped our political, social and economic world over the centuries.

Mastering Power

Nearly all men can stand adversity, but if you want to test a man's character, give him power.

Lincoln

Power tends to corrupt and absolute power corrupts absolutely.

Lord Acton

This deserves a special mention. Part of that animal nature, part of the human condition is a desire for power or control over our own destiny and of others. Even if we do not desire it, we seem to enjoy exercising it when we have it. You do not need to look at national leaders, millionaires or the barons of business. Go into any prison, any police station or walk through any passport control and watch

65

the behaviour of those who have power over others. It was Margaret Wheatley who said, 'When we think of ourselves as better than others, that is the beginning of tyranny.' Infamous experiments, such as the Stanford Prison Experiment, where a scenario was played out with young men randomly being given the role of prisoners and warders, show that few are immune to the misuse of that power when it is gained. The experiment had to be stopped after 6 days to prevent serious abuse and psychological damage from being done.

Recent research by Paul Piff in California into the impact of wealth and privilege show that it is a part of our human animal nature to abuse power when we have it. It reinforces the results of the infamous Milligram Experiments after World War II, where participants were instructed to deliver electric shocks to people when they gave wrong answers.

Religion is far from immune. Whatever the philosophy, the origin and the purity of the initial teachings, those who follow frequently use it as a vehicle for imposing their will on others. To be high up in the hierarchy or institutions of such influence and power is very seductive to the ego, let alone to be the voice of God. Even those who see themselves as progressive, enlightened, ethical exponents of political correctness seek to impose their own dogma on others.

You will be in a position of power at some stage in your life, perhaps great power. How will you handle it? Will you forget all this and slip easily into the seductive belief that it is your entitlement, the result of your intellect and talent rather than the great lottery of life.

Beware that, when fighting monsters, you yourself do not become a monster ... for when you gaze long into the abyss, the abyss gazes also into you.

Friedrich Nietzsche.

The Computer – Our incredible storage system

The computer, as Peters describes it, is permanently switched on, constantly scanning the world around us and taking on board the vast amount of sensory information available to us. It enables us to live much of our life on auto-pilot and it sorts and stores the information that we pass into it. The instinctive, animal mind, or the chimp, is triggered into action where there is any kind of a potential threat or to meet other physiological needs such as hunger and sex. It is far faster and stronger than our 'human' mind and so, if we are to develop personal mastery then we need to learn how to manage these different elements of our self.

Much of our life can easily be spent in 'auto-pilot', responding to either our own internal 'programmes' or the overt or subtle pressures of the external world. We will make countless decisions without testing the factors that are influencing us; beliefs developed through our unique upbringing and social pressures. Many of those beliefs are what can be called 'self-limiting', in that they impose artificial constraints on our thinking and, thus, our behaviour. 'I can't' or 'I mustn't' are statements based on perceptions and values that have, in our minds, become fact and dogma.

Programming the Computer

Developing mindfulness, the awareness and understanding of our thoughts and feelings can enable us to master them and to choose our responses with more freedom. I will talk more about mindfulness later but I cannot stress just how important it is as a practice to develop personal mastery. We need to learn how to re-programme the computer so that it supports the way that we want to live our life rather than the instinctive, animal impulse. We also need to learn how to manage that chimp – knowing when to listen to it and when to quieten its fears. I have included a framework at Annex B where you can look more closely at those beliefs that lie in your own computer – beliefs about yourself, about others, about work, about God about all things.

The Whole Self – the higher self

Chimp, human and computer – is that it? When we talk about the whole self, the authentic self, the higher self, what does that mean? What is this 'self'? We have personality tests, we can determine our motivations, our instincts and measure our emotional and cultural intelligence but these are only small parts of our self.

Michael Singer, in his book *The Untethered Soul*, takes us through a wonderful process of stripping away all the transient elements of our worldly life, all the labels we use to build our persona, our identity in the world. When we are asked, 'who are you?', we normally respond with our name. We are far more, though, than a jumble of letters given to us by our parents. We might go on to describe ourselves as the father or mother of our children or another role we play. Perhaps we would describe our experiences in life. Again, though, we are more than this; we would still exist without any of those things, so who are we? When we can stop the chattering voices in our mind, rid ourselves of the clutter and baggage we have accumulated through our lives, we reveal our deepest sense of self, of consciousness, the inner being: the 'one who sees'.

Inner Work

This inner journey to the very essence of you is a powerful experience. It can take many forms: the ancient practices of pilgrimage, the labyrinth walk and silent retreats. There is a guided meditation at Annex B for you but if that is not enough, or you do not feel comfortable with this inner work on your own, either get in touch or seek guides who can help on this journey. The New Age has prompted many souls to help others on this path.

Ancient Wisdom Meets Quantum Theory

I have found the Vedic traditions of Ancient India to provide the most useful framework for understanding our nature. This ancient wisdom describes the human being as a dynamic energy system, with that energy flowing around the body and intersecting at certain points in the body to form 'wheels' of energy. In the tantric texts they are described as emanations of consciousness from Brahman, an energy emanating from the spiritual and gradually becoming form, creating these distinct levels of energy. These wheels or *chakras* vibrate at different rates, emit different colours on the spectrum and reflect different aspects or dimensions of our self.

In the Western world, dominated by intellect and our drive to analyse, define and control, we too easily neglect or ignore those aspects of our self that defy logic and cannot be easily measured. As science has evolved, though, it is becoming more aligned with esoteric science and traditional Eastern philosophies. Quantum physics has demonstrated how we are, at the atomic and sub-atomic levels, simply bundles of dynamic energy. Modern health workers also now describe the human body as a dynamic energy system.

Bringing the Knowledge to Life

Developing this 'whole being' is hardly a new idea. The ancient Essenes of Palestine based their lives on it. They recognised seven heavenly forces and seven earthly forces within us. They developed an understanding of these energies, focused on developing them and used them to direct their daily life and patterns of working in accordance with the natural laws that govern our universe.

So, I have taken these ancient philosophies and 'twisted the kaleidoscope' to meet my needs here. In doing so, I have brought in my own understanding and interpretation of what these energy centres represents in the way of personal mastery. I have labelled each dimension with a word beginning with I (and there is some poetic licence here as you will see), and with the integration of those dimensions comes more I's, a sense of Integrity and Identity.

THE DIMENSIONS OF MASTERY

Each of the seven dimensions relates to a specific chakra. Each has a positive and negative, a light and a shadow and, as they are part of a dynamic energy field, they each impact on all the others. They are at the same time both separate and inextricably interwoven.

Instinctive Mind

This dimension is linked to the Kundalini or m?l?dh?ra chakra and is the primal life force. It is located at the base of the spine and is associated with survival, the will to live and our instinctive nature. It manifests in our competitive nature, our physical desires and energy levels. It feeds our strength of ambition and determination to succeed. It will manifest in our reaction to a perceived threat and conflict; our 'fight or flight' instinct. On the shadow side, if we allow this energy to grow too strong, it will lead to greed and excessive fear. The positive attributes of competition and ambition, of determination and forcefulness can, if unfettered, become combative, bullying behaviours.

Intimacy

This dimension is based on the Sacral or sv?dhih?na chakra and represents the feeling dimension – the area of emotion, of sexual energy and the creative force that links us to others. It is located just below your 'tummy button' and is the dimension of relationships with people and the world around us, and our feelings provide us with the ability to 'intimate' a situation, to feel into a situation or event and empathise with others. If this area is blocked by memories or other dimensions then relationships, warmth and empathy may be a problem, but it can also be too open and lead to over-indulgence and naivety. This area of relationships is a vital one in our lives - just take a moment to think how relationships have impacted on our lives, from birth through to the grave. There is an argument, based on quantum theory, that 'nothing exists except in relationship to everything else', and even Sun Tzu suggested in his *Art of War* 4000 years ago if we know ourself and we know the person we are working with, then we can choose the right approach in any situation or with any group or individual.

Intellect

I have labelled the next dimension, relating to the solar plexus chakra, as Intellect. Traditionally this is that the dimension that gives us our sense of identity - perhaps ego is the term that might be used here - and it holds a powerful grip on our lives. Together with the instinctive mind, this dimension has shaped more than any other the modern business world. I have labelled it intellect as I see this as the dimension of our physical mind. Far from a purely rational mind, however, this energy holds mental models from our history, conscious and unconscious and from the culture that we have grown up in. This dimension enables us to make sense of the world, quickly when necessary.

The shadow side is the prejudice and assumptions that will dictate our actions and often lead to conflict. From birth, we develop a set of beliefs, attitudes and behaviours to defend, reinforce and grow our sense of identity and self. Our instinctive fear will be triggered by a threat to our sense of self-esteem or identity. And, so we will create a powerful defensive system to defend our identity, beliefs, attitudes and the behaviours that spring from them.

Interconnection

Interconnectedness is the next dimension and is the bridge in our development as a person between the physical and emotional levels of consciousness to the mental and spiritual dimension. This is the area of the heart or an?hata chakra, and is associated with love, devotion and service. As energy, love is the binding force of the universe; it is an expression of the Divine Feminine that enables light to come into form. It is this dimension that gives us a sense of the whole, of being part of something greater than I – and it is the development of this dimensions that helps us to master and break away from the 'lower' instinctive and intellectual dimensions that preserve our own ego and limited sense of identity. It leads to a sense of unity, compassion and belonging. In my leadership work, this is the dimension that underpins the concept of servant leadership and the importance of service that brings a sense of social responsibility. The opening and full expression of this energy I see as vital to transform our modern business world and enable the higher dimensions to come more into our way of living and working.

I-xpression

I-xpression is the dimension relating to the throat or vi?uddha chakra, and is all about what and how we communicate, how we choose and express our words, our actions, our work. It is the area where we decide what we show to the outer world and what we keep hidden – the area that encompasses the whole concept of authenticity. Do we wear a mask and play a role or do we express our true, authentic nature? This dimension is closely linked to the idea of creativity, how we express that aspect of ourselves and equally important, the idea of humility. Humility is vital for mastery. By humility I do not mean self-effacement or shy modesty.

Humility comes from knowing yourself and from knowing your

place in the great scheme of things. There is always the danger of losing our balance of course - within each dimension and on the journey as a whole. We can acknowledge our light and greatness and lose sight of our shadow and our insignificance. We can be overwhelmed by our insignificance and our darkness and lose sight of the light and the greatness that sits within us.

Intuition

Intuition is the dimension that is linked to the brow or ?jñ? chakra, often referred to as the Third Eye. This is the inner voice and the channel to higher wisdom. It gives us the clarity of judgement that we use to make sense of all the data our senses give us. It gives us the sense of rightness that we use to test our thoughts and actions beyond our instinctive or intellectual mind. These will often fight against this intuition - this deep voice of the soul. For me this is another of the most important dimensions to develop if we are to develop the kind of character that will provide for our spiritual as well as physical needs. It will enable us to know the difference between our prejudices, our beliefs, our instinctive reaction and the clear sense of rightness.

Inspiration

Inspiration is linked to the crown or sahasr?ra chakra and is associated with our link to the higher worlds. In the past, this channel of inspiration has been provided by the shaman figure who would sit alongside the king who, incidentally, would be wearing the crown - a symbol of this link to the higher dimensions. When active and flowing, it provides a sense of meaning and purpose, the reassurance and guidance that we are aligned with our own soul, purpose. The root of the word is *spirere*, to breathe. The same source as for the word 'spirit'. And this is the meaning that I choose to use for this dimension. It is an acceptance and understanding of a source of wisdom beyond the material world, beyond the third-dimensional world. This energy touches the deepest part of our being and can promote an intensity of devotion and worship beyond any physical form. The shadow, though, is dangerous. The sense of a divine power in ourselves can be seductive; the temptation to abuse that power is strong.

Integrity

The meaning of the word 'yoga' in Sanskrit is to join, to connect or to unify. The dimensions weave together, each impacting on the others and our aim is to harmonise those energy centres and to connect our individual selves with the universal consciousness. So it is with my model. For me, integrity is not just about honesty and morality, it is linked to the word 'integer', which means whole and it is a state of being that approaches whole-ness or perhaps even holiness. It is the place from which I stand, whole, authentic and expressing my own truth, but in way that is in accord with the great principles that govern our universe. The foundation, or perhaps the final goal of personal mastery, is to become whole.

Mastery involves an acknowledgement that we embody all these dimensions, all at the same time regardless of age or maturity. In this physical life, we will not lose our instinctive nature, nor are we ever without those 'higher' dimensions that mark us apart from the animal forms around us.

The Weaving Patterns of Energy

Over-dominance of the energy in one area will lead to a block or imbalance in others, quite possibly leading to inappropriate behaviour and physical, emotional or mental ailments. When we allow fear and greed to become dominant, they will block our capacity for compassion, for communication and for listening to the voice of 'higher wisdom'. If we allow the higher dimensions to become too dominant, we may lose touch with reality or become fanatical in our faith or beliefs. Mastery comes when we are aware of and understand these dimensions within us and how they impact on each other. Then we can control and choose our thoughts, words and actions.

The Energy Field of Trust

Awareness of our inner world helps us in the outer world. We can see that our relationships are part of a multi-dimensional, multi-layered energy field involving our own dimensions and the multiple energies of each other person. The more aware we are of this, the better able to create an atmosphere and a way of working and living that builds understanding and trust.

These dimensions within us are like a kaleidoscope; their influence on us changes minute by minute, situation to situation. Nothing is black and white. There is a need to live with paradox and ambiguity, to accept each other as we are, if we are to develop deeper levels of trust – in relationships and in organisations.

Humility is the Key

The ability to harmonise the dimensions depends on our sense of humility. Humility is not modesty. Humility is holding, at the same moment, the knowledge of our immense power and greatness together with our miniscule significance within the great cosmos around us. It is built on the knowing that the source of all our power, the universal consciousness, is open to all. It is not a restricted domain.

When we become fully aware of this potential within ourselves and in others, then we become more open to learning and to supporting others in their learning too.

Inner and Outer Worlds

Working to master the energy within us enables us to evolve, but also automatically brings us into an awareness and understanding of the world in which we live and how to transform that world. Together, the dimensions hold the meaning and purpose to all life.

Each dimension must be balanced by all the others. The drive, empathy and practicality. The sense of unity that comes from the heart, the sense of humility that comes from an understanding of our true nature and the sense of rightness that comes from our intuition. I have included a table capturing these dimensions at Annex B to help in assessing your current state in each one.

Now that we have a better idea of our vehicle, its potential and its limitations, we can move on to the next stage of planning our journey.

Direction and Discipline

WHO WILL I BE?

The Whole Picture

Now that we have a clearer idea of the mountain and the nature of the challenge we face, we can begin to look for a path to take us to higher levels of consciousness. To help define this way of being, we need to look at the physical, the emotional, the mental and the spiritual - the whole self. All is one; the same principle applies to each individual as to the whole cosmos. I know this from my own experience. I know the impact of my physical fitness on my mental sharpness, the impact of a small toothache on my emotional balance, the impact of any anxieties on my sleep patterns and, from that, my physical and emotional state.

You may decide that you want to be healthier and adjust your diet to lose some excess weight, but if you have not also looked at your exercise regime, if you haven't considered how to deal with the conflicts that are causing so much stress and encouraging you to eat more, if you haven't created the time in your schedule for rest and relaxation, then your new diet will go the way of all those other new resolutions. To walk this path requires a review and reframing of your whole life.

In Ancient Egypt there was no word for religion. Spirit was interwoven in every aspect of life - there was no need for a separate word. I like the quote from Albert Schweizer, who said,

'My work is my life, my life is my work'.

Following this idea, every aspect of our lives becomes an expression of our spiritual impulse.

Balance and Harmony

The intention is not to plan every last detail of your lives. After all, the expression, 'When man plans, God laughs', is based on hard-won experience. However, it makes sense to me to step back from the path at intervals - maybe annually, maybe monthly or daily depending on our personality - to check that we are moving in the right direction. It makes sense to me to reflect for a while on how I want to spend my time in this precious life, doing the things that are important to me. Good intentions and a vague sense of what a good life might be, is easy - doing it, living it, that is not so easy. It requires discipline and planning.

As we weave this great tapestry, let's begin with the main threads on which our life will hang.

A Clear Purpose and Direction

We have been talking about the purpose of life and the nature of this great oneness that we are a part of. Now we need to determine our own purpose in this life. This sense of purpose, of some higher path to follow, might be thought to be the domain of religions and all mapped out for us already. Aside from the spiritual quest, a sense of purpose also gives meaning and energy to our lives. It inspires us - in all walks of life.

The Power of Purpose

Field Marshal Bill Slim, one of the greatest British soldiers who fought in World War II and a great philosopher of leadership, described the three elements of leadership as the physical, mental and spiritual, 'Of which, by far the most important is the spiritual,' he said. 'And by spiritual, I do not mean any religion or faith, I mean the sense of striving for a purpose greater than yourself.'

I remember it was in 1981, just a few months after joining my first unit in the army, sitting around a great fire with the soldiers, enjoying a beer before the final week's test exercise in northern West Germany. Towards the end of the evening, my boss, the unit commander, called for quiet and began to tell a story. As a young rookie, I didn't quite know how to react – storytelling didn't seem quite right for us tough soldiers. It was a story about how, in times of old, a war was lost all for the sake of a horse shoe nail. He described how, in those great battles of the past, the king would sit on a hill watching the deployment of the armies and then, at the critical moments, send messengers to his own troops. In this battle, as the king saw the enemy infantry splitting, he sent a messenger away to launch his cavalry to make the decisive strike.

I was looking around the faces of the soldiers to see what their reaction was. They were transfixed – they knew this man better than I did. Anyway, as the messenger rode towards the cavalry, a nail came out of the horse's shoe. The shoe came loose and fell off, the horse was injured by a stone and could not move any further. The message was not passed, the cavalry did not charge, the battle was lost and the war was lost – all for the sake of a horseshoe nail.

'So, why am I telling you this story?' I remember his words – and I remember my own thoughts, 'Yes, why are you telling this story?' He went on, 'I'll tell you why. Over the next few days, when you are cold and tired, you may think of yourself as that horseshoe nail, small and insignificant. Your actions will make no difference, there is no live enemy out there and it will not matter whether you fall asleep or perform each action to the best of your ability. Well, let me tell you why it is important. The Soviets are watching us. They will be watching to see what they will face if they step across that border. Our professionalism over these next seven days may be the difference between the Soviets launching an assault on our countries or not. And why does that matter? It matters to you, Sergeant Smith, to keep your two little daughters safe. It matters to you, Bombardier Jones, because it will keep your beloved Liverpool football club alive and safe.' He picked out two or three more individuals and then finished by saying, 'You may think of yourself as that horseshoe nail, but you are much more than that. Each one of us is a part of something very special; we are here for our families for a way of life that we love. Over the next seven days look after each other, but you also have my permission to kick each other up the backside if you think that they fall below the standards we expect.' I may have missed out some of the choicer words but you get the message. And, so did we. Nobody spoke for what seemed like an age and as I looked around the faces in the darkness, every eye was on him. He had touched something deep inside us. It was a powerful lesson for this young soldier.

In his book *Man's Search for Meaning*, Viktor Frankl tells the incredible story of his time in Auschwitz and Dachau. One of the profound insights from this experience was the importance to all of us, as human beings, of the sense of purpose and meaning in our work and lives. With it, as he describes, we can endure the unimaginable. Without it, we can, quite literally, give up and die. That purpose may be to live life in a way that is linked perhaps to a spiritual belief or a faith. For Frankl, it was to survive so he could continue his work; very often that sense of purpose will be linked to the work we do. That is why so many die soon after they retire.

Finding our Purpose

So, these are the big questions that we rarely take time out to answer. Who am I? Why am I here? What is the purpose of my life? What do I want to achieve in my work and life? What legacy will I leave? Who will I be and how will I live my life?

There is a famous speech given to graduates at Stanford by Steve

Jobs, the founder of Apple. He talks about his own experience and how, sometimes, you can only see the meaning and purpose in your life when you look back and 'join up the dots'. It's an idea worth exploring and links to the idea that all is as it should be, and we are in the right place at the right time, that we are guided by forces beyond our understanding and are always given the training and resources to meet the challenges we face.

So, explore looking backwards. There are some simple questions that you can ask yourself and then spend time contemplating. What are your strengths and the talents that you have been given? What do you love to do, recognising that it may not be what you are doing or working on now? What do you feel drawn to in the world right now - what cause touches something within you?

This is work for the 4th Space and, when you have spent time in reflection and meditation, capture your own sense of purpose in words or in a picture or a symbol. There is also a guided meditation at Annex B which you can use to explore.

CLEAR GUIDING PRINCIPLES AND VALUES

A value: *'an enduring belief that a specific way of being is personally or socially preferable to opposite or converse way of being'.*

We all have values; they are embedded in our different cultures and taught to us from birth. They help us to navigate the world and they direct our attitudes and behaviour. They also help us to make choices in life which will develop a sense of integrity and trustworthiness; a sense of wholeness and completeness - of living your values and respecting those of others. When you live with integrity, your actions are congruent with your words; your words reflect your true thoughts and feelings. You develop a character rich in inner strength, self-worth, maturity, and an abundance mentality will radiate genuineness and a sense of trustworthiness. You develop true courage, knowing what is in your heart and being prepared to stand for it.

'Ultimately it is our values that provide the stars by which we navigate through life.'

Another person's map will be different to our own; we are all shaped by the world we are born into. Now is a time to detach yourself for a moment from the path that you have followed to this point in time and choose again the values and principles that will enable you to be who you wish to be. This might be an area of discomfort – you might see it as 'trying to change my personality'. In a way, I am trying to do that. I want to encourage you to develop and nurture certain dimensions of your persona and to loosen the grip of others.

This is a challenging task, not least because of our nature. Our computer is programmed with many stories about the world and with many beliefs about our self and others. They are fed to us from our birth, by parents, teachers, priests and anyone who holds influence over us. Many of those beliefs lie in our unconscious and impact on our words and actions without us realising. We may be more aware of the idea of prejudice and bias nowadays but it does not lessen their hold. Many of those beliefs and stories we may choose to keep in our lives, but we do need to consciously choose rather than simply accept them from others. There is an exercise in Annex B, which can help you to test and clear the beliefs that you hold – about yourself, about others and other cultures or religions, about work, about life and death.

Certain principles govern all effective human relationships. Some are based on our instinctive nature: the need to survive, the 'selfish gene'. Others are based on concepts that spring from a different part of our nature such as truth, love, peace and honesty. We have a capacity for acts of great kindness and generosity – even sacrificing our lives for others or a great cause. We also have a capacity for acts of selfishness and violence – abusing others or killing others for our own gain or in service of a 'great' cause. People of great wealth can be extremely self-centred, people in great poverty or suffering can be incredibly generous. There are no racial, ethnic, gender differences in these fundamental characteristics – only in how we learn or choose to deploy them.

I have created my own set of principles and have included these in Annex A as an example of how you might approach creating your own 'compass'. You will see that there are no new insights, that is not the aim here. It is through this process of taking personal ownership of our deepest thoughts, and then the actions springing from them, that we will give ourselves the will and the discipline to bring them to life. There is an exercise in Annex B which might help you to determine your own guiding values and principles, translating them into words and actions that are meaningful to you. This is more 4th Space work. When these are clear, capture them in words or symbols and then we can move onto the next stage of this preparatory work, creating your own code.

OUR PERSONAL CODE

The Compass to Keep Us on the Path

As we have seen, we are incredible beings; evolving from the animal kingdom, we retain those survival and nurturing instincts alongside our rational mind and higher consciousness. Despite all our scientific and cultural achievements, though, all human beings face the same challenge, to be guided in our words and actions by instinct or by that higher nature.

Over the centuries, we have struggled to control our instinctive, selfish nature and we have struggled to deal with power. It is rare to see the self-discipline that is needed to master those instincts and, even in the great temples and monasteries, we have needed an external discipline to help us keep to the path we have chosen. In my army days, I learnt that we achieve self-discipline invariably through an imposed discipline – whether on the battlefield, the sports field or in the classroom. It begins with a clear code of behaviour – a set of guiding rules or principles against which we can test our daily decisions, words and actions.

Writing Your Own Code

Have a look at the laws of chivalry and the Ten Commandments. They are examples of a code drawn up for groups following their path. You will see there are some themes and some big differences. Take your time in creating your own code, based on your own philosophy and principles. It is your compass on the mountain, your reference when the mist and darkness make the path hard to follow.

Druss the Legend – My Inspiration

I have also been inspired by others – and not just those from an overtly spiritual calling. One source has been the writing of author David Gemmell. His genre is not religion or sacred texts but heroic fantasy and, in his books, he captures so much of the human story; the battle between good and evil both in the outer world and the inner world. One of his heroes is Druss the Legend, and Druss lived his life in accordance with his 'iron code'.

In his code, and in his own words, he challenges himself to always respect women and children, to protect the weak against abuse and never to lie, cheat or steal. He commits to never allowing personal greed to tempt him away from his path or fear to prevent him confronting an enemy. He finishes by saying that words are not enough. Saying 'I will not be evil' is not enough; he demands that evil must be fought wherever it is found.

Make it Meaningful

Make it meaningful to you. You may choose to use symbols or pictures to capture your thoughts. Over the years, I have used different symbols to remind me of the path I have chosen and my values. My code, titled the Gentle Warrior, is also included in Annex A. I carry it with me in my own journal and I look at it often. It has become, for me, a spiritual practice to carry it with me and a recognition that I need a constant reminder to keep to the path. It may not be as 'catchy' as I would like but, over the years, it has been a compass for the choices I have made in my daily life.

Look for the highest values and character within yourself – do the Values Exercise that is included in Annex B and read again the Eightfold Path. I have included a list of potential behaviours or commitments here, drawn from a variety of sources and re-shaped in my own words.

DEFINING OUR CODE

Integrity, Honesty and Trustworthiness.

In my work in developing leadership, I have come to view it as a way of travelling with people rather than being a position of authority. You can see that the idea of travelling on a journey is a bit of a theme with me. In many ways, the development of that kind of leadership is similar to this spiritual journey. And, on every list of qualities that has been produced to describe great leadership, the words integrity, honesty and trustworthiness invariably appear at the top of the list.

Example is not the main thing in influencing people, it is the only thing.

There is no shortcut to developing those qualities and, even worse news, they can so easily be lost or damaged by a single lapse. There is no quick fix or off the shelf package. We have come to expect easy solutions in our modern society but the development of integrity and trustworthiness requires sacrifice, discipline, total application and a lifetime's work.

Principles to Live By

Below are some ideas that you might include in your personal code – defining the way that you wish to live your life. The first are from my Reiki practice. Reiki (pronounced ray-key) is a Japanese word meaning Universal Life Energy, an energy which is all around us. It is the name given to a system of natural healing which evolved in Japan from the experience and dedication of Dr Mikao Usui (d. 1926).

Just for today do not worry.
Just for today do not anger.
Honour your parents, teachers and elders.
Earn your living honestly.
Show gratitude to every living thing.

I like the last principle very much. It is a great practice – that's not to say it is easy – to constantly remind ourselves of our place in the great, ever changing, circle of life.

Here are some more ideas:

Do no harm. I am sure that you will have heard of a similar mantra. 'Do no harm to others' is accredited first to Hippocrates, the Ancient Greek physician. I like the idea of just 'doing no harm'; we have caused so much pain and damage to our planet and other forms of life that we need to change our selfish ways. Focusing on people, though, I suggest that it should include not using unkind, negative or violent words. This is hard, especially when you are tired, under pressure or want to release your frustration or anger. Just think how many times you are drawn into gossip where you use unkind words about others. It is becoming increasingly hard in the modern age, with the corrosive effect of social media where we are bombarded with opinions and allegations, often unfounded, about others.

Swearing and blasphemy have become everyday language in my country. The words we use, unthinkingly, are an uncontrolled expression of violent emotion. They bring that violence into the world - stop it. I love the quote,

> *'Do not speak unless your words are more beautiful than the silence.'*

Through this discipline - of not using these negative or violent words - you are demonstrating personal mastery, the Buddhist principle of Right Words and the principle of respect for all. It links to the practice below of looking for the best in others.

Stop, Look, Listen, Think. Then Act. This is another expression of living mindfully. Constantly remind yourself to pay attention to the world and people around you and your own inner world. Develop the habit of making your words and actions the 'right' ones and not just instinctive responses.

This is a practice to develop patience with others and reduce conflict. It is hard at times of stress, and that is when it matters the most. We may say the wrong things but also become sullen and withdraw; each course serves to damage relationships. You can practise this in the car too – each time you are tempted to slam your hand onto the horn, just stop and ask yourself, 'Will my action help here?'

In 1996, I was driving with my son along a road in Tunbridge Wells. I stopped to let another car come out of a side street. I waited for the expected wave of thanks – mandatory in the old English culture of politeness. Instead, I got a 'finger' (a sign of abuse) and a snarling face hurling what looked like abuse through the car windscreen. I slammed my hand down on the horn. My son looked up at me – he was just nine years old – and asked in a quiet voice, 'Why did you hoot the horn like that, Daddy?' I had recovered my composure and explained how Daddy was angry with the woman and her rude gesture. My son ripped away my attempt at maturity with the words, 'I can understand why you might be angry, Daddy, but I don't think that hooting the horn really helped.'

It is said that our children are our greatest teachers. Since that day, I have consciously not used my horn – even, at times, when it was more than justified. I have seen it as a personal practice to help master that instinct to anger and rage.

Look for the Golden. Look beyond the behaviour, look beyond the physical body and see the gold that sits within. This practice will help you to see the difference between the person, the inner self and their behaviour. This is challenging but, as a practice, it benefits us in two ways. First, it helps us to master our own prejudices and emotions. Rather than muttering expressions like 'typical of him,' or 'those people, that's just like them,' by being very specific about the behaviour and identifying the reasons why it causes an emotional reaction we can keep a more balanced perspective.

Second, while we need to deal with bad behaviour, by focusing on the person behind the behaviour and all that has led to it we will be in a better position to support change and to build in others a sense of self-esteem. Developing the ability to identify the specific behaviour that is causing the negative reaction and then to give effective, constructive feedback is a powerful practice.

Assume the best of others. Our judgements are often projections of our own fears or beliefs. People will also tend to respond to how we treat them.

Small Acts of Kindness. Whenever we do good for others, without the motive of impressing others, we increase our own sense of self-worth and respect. Our modern world encourages us to self-publicise, to seek acclaim – finding ways to step off the path to narcissism and selfishness is important. In one book, I came across the idea of 'picking up worms'. Taking worms from the road and placing them in the hedge beside the road. No fuss, no selfies, no great impact on the world – just a selfless service to another seed of life sharing this world. Try it and notice any feelings that arise from the act.

Serenity, Courage and Wisdom. My grandmother gave a beautiful glass ornament with the inscription:

> *God grant me the serenity to accept the things I cannot change, the courage to change things I can, and the wisdom to know the difference.*

It is easy to complain and spread our negativity. It is easy to step back and avoid confrontation or the condemnation of others. By avoiding wasteful 'whingeing' we are not drawn into the negativity. By acting we accept personal responsibility, refusing to blame others and circumstances. Of course, we need to be aware of our surroundings and the dangers of the world but it is too easy to justify away our inaction. Do the right thing!

All is Perfect – Accept it. This builds on the idea of developing the serenity to accept things as they are. Like the other practices, it is so easy to say. First, accept yourself. Accept and acknowledge your mistakes and flaws. Accept your fears, listen to them and acknowledge them. Recognise when you argue simply from the compulsive need to defend, justify or attack - and stop. Second, accept others and their situation. By accepting them as they are, you are affirming their worth as a human being.

Then, if you can accept both yourself and others as they are, without judgement and comparison, then you no longer need to try to make yourself look better or feel stronger - no more need for bullying, for abuse, for discrimination, for unkindness. Margaret Wheatley said, 'When we think of ourselves as superior to others, then begins tyranny.'

My Word is Sacred. Our ability to make and keep promises is a measure of our integrity. It is so easy to make promises which either we are not able to keep or we forget. 'Everything will be alright. I promise.' Each time you say that, and everything is not alright, you lose more of the trust of others.

Be Here Now. Be more present - in the moment. As we focus on doing something positive about the things that we can control our circle of influence expands. This relates to the practice of mindfulness and I will cover this in more depth in Annex B. For me, this is a practice which has a profound impact on our state of mind, on our relationships and on our lives.

Choose Love. 'Love thy neighbour' - it's not a new idea but, goodness, how hard to implement. There are no absolutes in this world but, generally, people have a need to be valued, to belong and to be loved. We know where the quest for status and power leads us, we also have many examples of people who have lived a life based on love, caring, kindness, compassion and service. Choose love!

Tame the Tigers. Remember from earlier the Chinese story about the two tigers within us. Stop or dissolve the negative thoughts or emotions when they arise or when you hear them in others. Recognise where they come from – the stored memories and stories in your computer – but do not follow them, do not feed them; let them go and replace them with positive, loving thoughts.

Test All That You See, Hear, Speak or Do. I mentioned this practice, inspired by the Buddha, in the introduction. In a world of competing information sources, seek wisdom above propaganda. Accept nothing or nobody at face value. Explore, research, observe and listen. Enlarge your perspective: see the whole world as your home. Learn the difference between headlines and trends, between spin and substance.

See Yourself in Others, Hear Yourself in Their Voice. There is a great expression, 'We cannot love or hate something in another which does not reflect something that we love or hate in ourselves.' This 'rule' also reminds us that we are all part of the whole, all from the same source.

Hold to the Centre. Life is full of conflict. Even small things can disturb our balance and raise emotions. It is easy to let the chimp decide our course of action – fight or flight. Develop the ability to stay balanced, to explore the differences, to listen and to see other perspectives than your own. By holding to the centre, you develop a balance within yourself and the ability to help others see another, different perspective. You become a bringer of peace.

PERSONAL VISION

We have looked at the map, the nature of the mountain we are seeking to climb and the nature of the vehicle we are travelling in – this body, this life. Now, we can begin to create a vision of what real fulfilment will look like and feel like. We can define where we are we heading on this journey. It is not a place or a goal, it is who we will come to be through this incredible life experience.

I am going to ask you to live with some ambiguity here. Some will say that we don't need a vision; life is about the here and now. I have just suggested to you that mindfulness is a life-changing practice – and now I ask you to envision the future. We are all different and my experience is that a vision of who and what we might be (personally or collectively) can inspire people from all cultures and from all times. It ensures that, while we may live mindfully, day to day, we are heading in the right direction. It worked for me and I have used it with many others. It is one of the core dimensions of leadership – at all levels and including leading the self. If it doesn't work for you, leave it – but maybe think about a couple of things. Giving yourself a clear direction, striving for something meaningful, gives a sense of purpose and energy to all that you do. That can be inspiring not just for you but also others who know you. Just 'being,' suits the animal inside us and the enlightened soul that we seek to become but, for me, I find the idea of achieving what you set out for in life immensely satisfying and fulfilling. It is the 'middle way' and a stepping stone to our evolution.

My experience, my studies and research at establishments such as Yale Business School also suggest that by writing down a vision or a goal, or capturing it in an image or symbol, you will make it happen. If you don't, you are much less likely to. I wrote my first personal vision in 1992 – set for the year in 2000. Around 1998, I was feeling that I was just about there and needed to look to a new horizon – I set my next vision for 2006, then 2012 and then 2020. A vision should not be too close and not too far away as it loses meaning and power. It should be challenging and inspiring – this is the incentive for the struggles on the path you have chosen.

The vision quest is a rite of passage for the Native Americans. Four days of isolation and introspection in the wilderness to determine how they will use their medicine or power in the service of the community. That may seem to be a massive investment of time and effort in our modern world of instant communication and gratification, but it might help show us how important this exercise can be. Taking the time to set the direction for this precious life, to choose the path that we will walk on the mountain: that seems important to me.

I once heard a story on a workshop dealing with risk. One of the great barriers to taking risk is the fear of failure and this story was describing how a very successful (after many failed attempts) entrepreneur dealt with that fear. He described his own fear of failure as reaching the gates of heaven after he had died, imagining himself standing in front of St Peter and meeting there the person he might have been. For him, to not have tried, to have given up the chance of success just to stay safe, that was failure and that is what drove him on.

The vision should not be so far in the distance or so over-whelmingly challenging that it demotivates rather than inspires. Nor should it be so close in time and to where you are now that you hardly need to do more than what you are doing now to achieve it. The exercise, in Annex B, encourages you to envision a number of dimensions of your life – your health and fitness, your relationships, your work and how you express your talents, your role in the community and so on.

If you decide to use it, I suggest that you create a time and space for this exercise. Again, the 4th Space, but make this a special time – the vision quest. I set aside two days each year, one around the summer solstice and one around the winter solstice to review my own vision, my Wheel of Life and the coming year. It has become, for me a spiritual practice.

THE WHEEL OF LIFE

Now we have set the long-term vision and given ourselves the compass to keep us on the path, we can turn our attention to the daily and weekly activities that will make up our new way of life.

Discipline Is Not the Enemy of Freedom

I talked about the value of my army experience and this was a vital lesson; the critical role of discipline in creating an empowered individual or team. Without discipline, there is chaos. With discipline of mind, body and spirit, the conditions are created for freedom of expression, resilience in times of uncertainty and an inner sense of confidence.

I am going to share the tools that I have used to bring structure and discipline to my own life. They help to define how to use your precious time both in life and at work. You will see that they encourage a deeper thinking process; to reflect both on what activities are important in your life and, crucially, why they are important - what do they bring to your life? It is not about planning the details, it is about giving you a sense that you are living a full, meaningful life.

The Wheel of Life

The Wheel of Life can be used for your whole life and for specific elements, such as work. It can be used to bring balance into your life now or to move you towards a new way of living. The first stage is to identify the different roles or areas in your life that you already have or would like to have (it might be interesting to do one wheel for now and one for how you would like things to be - this will certainly give you an idea of what must change and how to create the space for the change).

Physical, Emotional, Mental and Spiritual

The example below has some ideas, but there is no set formula. The wheel will change as we go through life but it is good to have some checks and balances. Am I giving enough attention to each part - the physical, the emotional, the mental and spiritual? Am I caring for each of the dimensions of myself - from instinct to inspiration?

When my children were young, they had a separate spoke of the wheel. Now they are fully grown, I have moved them into my 'Family and Friends' area. I have always kept a separate area of 'Community', even though I consider it to be a big part of my spiritual life. It also feeds my emotional wellbeing.

Be Clear on Why They Are Important to You

The next stage is to write down your purpose for spending time in that area. It may sound strange to write a purpose for your relationships but this is important. By clarifying *why* this is important, you create a stronger incentive to ensure that you keep the balance right. If, as an example, you haven't really thought through how important your time with your children is, then it becomes easier for others to take that time away or for you to let it slip away. It also provides a check that you are spending your time on things that do matter.

When I completed my own Wheel of Life this helped me in a number of ways. Reflecting on why my work was important to me, I established a set of criteria against which I have tested my work for the last 28 years; Income, Impact and Enjoyment. By constantly asking the question, 'Why is that important to me?' I established just what impact I wanted my work to have, what kind of work I enjoyed and just how important the income was to me and my family. I was able to cut away the need to 'grow my business' just for the sake of it as it brought me no sense of enjoyment.

95

Reflecting on why the time with my children was important was also very helpful. Providing an income to support them was important but so was helping to provide a loving home, a loving relationship and a good education for life. It helped to get the most out of the time that we had together. Seeing the whole wheel gave me a sense of balance and took away the guilt if I was away from home working or enjoying a solitary run or game of golf. Each part of the wheel contributes to the whole.

Define the Way You Will Achieve Your Goals

The next stage is to determine the activities in each area that will move you towards your goal or achieve your purpose. At work, as an example, you may decide that you need to spend a certain amount of time coaching others or being coached, time studying or time preparing for meetings. The important thing is to be clear that it moves you towards your purpose. With my children in their early years I identified plenty of ways to spend time with my son – playing football and watching sport – but it was more challenging to find ways to be with my daughter. So, together we identified camping trips and theatre trips amongst other activities which would give us that time together.

Having identified the activities, you can plan your diary. It will never remain unchanged and there will be time lost and stolen from the different areas, but this wheel provides the check that things are in balance and the incentive to maintain that balance. It provides a visual display of how you are spending your time and a means to identify the areas that you need to give up or change.

You will notice that in the example below, there is a blank sector. I have always kept a space like that. It reflects a desire to remain open, willing to explore and make time for new activities and people.

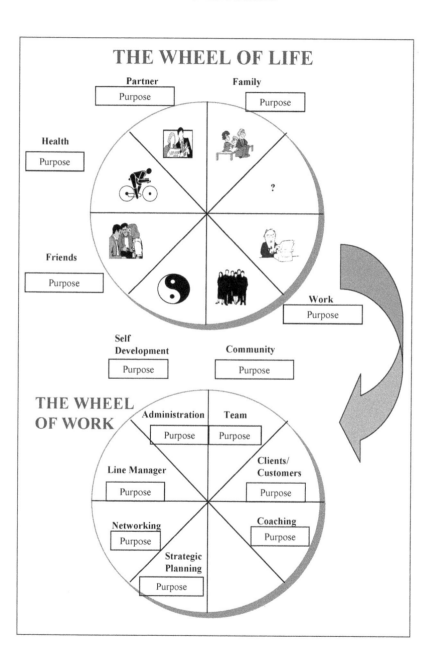

THE WHEEL OF LIFE

Work

Almost certainly, one part of your Wheel of Life will be about your work. Albert Schweizer, one of my great heroes from back in my childhood, wrote:

'My work is my life, my life is my work.'

I like that – especially 'my life is my work'. Work, whatever form it takes, is an expression of our talents, our sense of purpose and meaning. Bringing purpose and meaning to our work is life enriching – at every level. I do not hold to the limiting definition of work that we use in our modern society, or the even more insidious way that we place a value on it. A mother's work in raising her children is as important as the nuclear scientist's. An artist, a cleaner, a cook or a lawyer – each contributes to the social fabric, and who is to say which adds the most value?

We can use the same process for defining how we will spend our time to achieve our purpose at work, not only to be more efficient but also to know that everything we do has real meaning and purpose.

We work that we might keep pace with the Earth and the soul of
the Earth.
For when you are idle you become a stranger unto the seasons,
And step back from life's procession
Of majesty and suppressed pride toward the infinite.
When you work you are a flute through
Whose heart the whispering of the hours
Turns to music.
Which of you would be a reed, dumb and silent,
When all else sings together in unison?
Always you have been told that work is
A curse and labour a misfortune.

But I say to you that when you work you fulfil
A part of Earth's furthest dream, assigned to you
When the dream was born,
And in keeping yourself with labour you
Are in truth loving life,
And to love life's labour is to be intimate
With life's innermost secret.
And what does it mean to love work.
It is to weave a cloth with threads drawn from your own heart
For your beloved
It is to fill each thing you make or do with the breath of your
own spirit.

From *The Prophet* by Kahlil Gibran

Strengthening the Spirit

PRACTICES FOR THE JOURNEY AND THE WHEEL OF LIFE

You may decide, as Albert Schweizer suggested, that your whole life is your spiritual work. I feel the same. All our life is a spiritual experience; every word and act should be delivered with the right intention. Yet, I also acknowledge the power of rituals and spiritual practices to nurture and expand our state of consciousness.

I have always kept a part of my Wheel of Life for spiritual development and practice and I have enjoyed exploring rituals and spiritual practices from a range of traditions. I love the haka, the Maori ritual, that the All Blacks use to prepare themselves for battle - and to frighten the enemy. I love the chanting and incense in a church to create an atmosphere of reverence.

Rituals

Rituals help create a state of mind. They play an important part in our lives, from the form of greeting we use to the playing of the national anthem before big occasions. There is a danger, though, that they become too repetitive, lose their meaning and do not alter our state of consciousness. There is a balance to be struck between the discipline of simply performing a repetitive action and the joy and uplift that comes from a ritual performed mindfully and joyfully. So, even if you have your rituals in place, it is worth experimenting and refreshing this aspect of your spiritual life every now and then – to maintain their strength.

Discipline

Spiritual practices also can also develop discipline. The simple act of taking the time to conduct the practice – especially when the world demands us to be answering phones, texts, postings, preparing a report, making tea for the children – is a way of developing our willpower and self-discipline. The will is like a muscle; it can tire under continuous pressure but the more we exercise it, the stronger it gets. Without a strong will, we have no chance of mastering the instincts and emotions that constantly seek to take control.

Spiritual Practices

First, you can build on the work that we have already covered.

The 4th Space. Honour the divine part of your nature by creating a time and space to nurture it. Dedicate a time each day to stillness, to your inner work.

Develop a Learning Mindset. Adopt the learning cycle as a part of your work and your life. Spend time, regularly, reflecting on the lessons and insights from your own life experiences. Challenge the accepted belief that there are simply winners and losers. Learn, as Kipling said,

> *To treat these twin imposters just the same.*

An attitude which says, 'Whatever the outcome, I will learn and grow stronger and wiser,' leads to resilience and a sense of knowing that you can cope with whatever comes your way. It removes the idea of failure from your vocabulary.

Keep a journal as a way of deepening the learning experience. I kept a daily diary in the early days after I left the army – I had so much to learn, quickly. Now, I take time every few days to capture my state of mind and reflect on the lessons that I can take from what is happening. It has become a remarkably useful and enjoyable practice.

You do not need to limit yourself to writing. I carry a palette of watercolour paints and some brushes in my backpack and use them in my journal. I find that capturing my mood in colours and symbols is beautifully therapeutic. I studied the use of colour for healing at White Lodge and have enjoyed keeping it in my spiritual practice.

Define and Maintain Your Purpose, Principles and Code. This encourages you to reflect and contemplate deeply. It encourages you to see your own life in a different perspective and then to live life more mindfully and purposefully. The practice is to write it and to review it, to keep it as a living, evolving body of wisdom as you walk through life.

Staying open to new understanding is important. Attachment leads to fanaticism and the violence that we see all around us. Even if you follow a religion, I urge you to define the path for yourself – find the essence of the teachings rather than the layers of interpretation that have followed the great master who introduced it. Make this a ritual, a renewal of your commitment to the path that you have chosen.

Create and Maintain your Wheel of Life. This brings a sense of meaning to all that you are doing and will do.

Building the Spiritual Muscles

Now, look at the practices I have listed below and reflect on what energy they might bring into your life. Consider what might help open new levels of consciousness and bring joy into your life. They

102

might be expressed through daily routine, special times during the day, week, month, year, and life. You might look for support in a church or community or with a personal teacher, guide or facilitator. Certainly, for practices such as mindfulness and Qi Gong, it is a good idea to begin with a teacher who can help develop the habits – enabling you to have the skills to walk alone.

Honour Your Temple. Create and maintain a physical fitness regime based on way of life, environment, preferences and ambitions.

This may well be another complete section of your Wheel of Life, but I like the idea of making it a spiritual practice too. We have been given this precious body and mind to carry our soul and provide it with the vehicle for our evolution and for our service to the whole. It is the vehicle for all that we do in this life, and it makes sense to me to take care of it. To wash it, to feed and water it, to ensure it is strong and healthy as it can be in order to live our life to the full, what could be a more important spiritual practice? Psychologically, too, it has a positive impact to know that we are in the best shape we could be – not for the external admiration but for knowing that we can master the desires and temptations which so easily pull us off the path. Even our posture has an impact on our state of mind and our emotions.

As in all things, we need to look at the whole system and not just one part of it. As well as our diet and exercise regime, we need to consider all the aspects of our life. As an example, the kind of exercise regime that you will enjoy and be more likely to stick to can be influenced by your level of extroversion. Introverts will be much happier enduring the long runs or gym sessions on their own whereas, for the extroverts, company will greatly help them in enduring the suffering.

The choosing of a dietary regime that works for you – providing nourishment for the body, mind, emotions and the soul. Over the years I have tried and tested many regimes and, as well as keeping me in reasonably good shape, they provide a great exercise in willpower and self-discipline. Not eating when you are hungry – it's a constant challenge. When I left the army and began my healing work, I became a vegetarian. I didn't miss meat that much but, every time I walked past a fish and chip shop, I could smell the temptation.

I ate a 'food combining' diet for seven years and found it worked incredibly well for me – and others I introduced to it. I gave it up on the ultimatum of my wife, I had to choose; vegetarian or food combining, but not both. It does demonstrate the importance of considering each aspect of your life before you make these choices.

I have included some notes on physical fitness in Annex B. I loved the simplicity and effectiveness of running, especially cross-country, where I could also enjoy being in nature. With worn-out knees, I now do much more cycling and I have made the Chinese health exercises known as Qi Gong and Zang Zhaing, exercises for stretching and energy flow, a big part of my exercise regime. There are some more detailed notes on Qi Gong at Annex B too. The underlying philosophy as well as geographical roots are closely linked to yoga but I have found Qi Gong to be much more accessible and suitable for me than yoga – and the fact that it is less trendy also suits me well too.

So, you see, there is no 'one size fits all' and you can experiment with these different fitness practices until to find one that suits you.

Prayer. This is a traditional way to establish a connection with the higher dimensions. In the monotheistic religions, it is the way to connect directly with their God. You do not need to see God or the Source of Life as a separate entity from yourself to pray. As a ritual connection to the higher dimensions, I have used prayer to ask for healing, to ask for guidance from those souls who are close to me and for help when I have needed it.

*Heavenly Father, Mother Earth, Great Masters, The White
Brotherhood, The Essene Brotherhood and all those who know
and love me, thank you for bringing me here, thank you for
being here with me.
Please, today, grant me the wisdom, strength and courage to do
our work.
Help to be a centre of peace and a channel for light, love and
healing energy.
Help me to find the right words with each person that I meet, to
enable, inspire and encourage.
Help to be ever more in tune with the natural rhythms of
the universe that I may be who I came to be and do what I
came to do.*

I have prayed with the spirit of great oak trees, the ocean and to the
moon. I wouldn't publicise that in every walk of life but here I share
my own experience in the hope that it gives you the confidence to
explore and find your own way.

MINDFULNESS

This practice demands special attention from me. It lies at the very
heart of my own quest for personal mastery and of my work in
leadership development. It is a practice which touches every aspect
of our lives.

A Definition

Mindfulness means paying attention: on purpose, in the present
moment and non-judgementally to whatever arises in the field of
your experience. Its origins lie in Buddhist meditative traditions but

105

the mindfulness approach is swiftly moving into the mainstream of leadership, personal effectiveness, emotional intelligence and stress reduction.

The Evidence

Since 2001, controlled studies by Davidson, and Kabat-Zinn, have shown the impact of mindfulness training. They show that we can change the way our brain functions and, in doing so, change our physical and emotional state of being. Brain scans consistently show that mindfulness training increases activity in the left, pre-frontal cortex of the brain, the seat of positive thinking and happiness. It leads to greater engagement in their work, more energy and less anxiety. Research also shows that this training and the associated shift in brain activity improves the robustness of the immune system.

The Impact

How does this impact on our lives? In developing these qualities within ourselves, regardless of our position, we can inspire and make work and life enjoyable, however demanding it is. People who do this tend to be highly 'approach' oriented and positive rather than being a drain on the enthusiasm of teams and organisations. It encourages a resonance with those around you through self-awareness, self-management, social awareness, and relationship management. All are, to some extent, mindfulness skills.

Positions of responsibility, power and influence can leave people physically and emotionally drained. Even with the best of intentions, people can become closed and frustrated with others. Mindfulness training strengthens our openness and acceptance of others while developing our ability to manage our emotions and focus.

Mindfulness teaches you to take an interest in all aspects of one's experience and to treat it with acceptance and curiosity. It teaches you to embrace and understand each passing moment with warmth, care, and curiosity. As pressures increase, mindfulness will have an even greater impact on our ability to live a life of harmony and fulfilment.

Practices and a Schedule

As well as mindfulness practices (I have included a number of these and a schedule to help you create a programme in Annex B), adopt daily rituals to maintain a state of mindfulness through the day. At the beginning of the day, at meal times, before exercise, at the end of the day. Each or any meal, each mouthful of food can be a mindfulness or spiritual practice. A short prayer before the meal. A special meal each day or each week. Preparing yourself to sleep with a prayer or meditation. Any aspect of your daily routine can become a ritual practice. The benefit of adopting these small practices is that it enables you to live your life more mindfully and in a higher state of consciousness – pulling you out of the whirlpool of daily life.

MEDITATION

'The pause between two thoughts.'

'The process of getting to know myself completely, both who I am "inside" and how I react to what is "outside".'

'To experience a state of peace, just for a few moments.'

Why Meditate?

You can see from these descriptions that meditation is used for many different things. It is an ancient practice to still the mind – thus bringing physical relaxation but also the opportunity for fresh, creative or inspirational thoughts and ideas to emerge. It is used as a spiritual practice in many traditions as a gateway to the unconscious and to the higher dimensions. In my leadership work, it is a practice that can be used to develop the leadership qualities of inspiration, intuition and interconnection.

There are many books that you can read. I have found that my mindfulness practice, bringing my mind into a peaceful state, has been of great benefit to my deeper, meditative practice. They are different, mindfulness and meditation, although the former can be a gateway to the latter. Mindfulness is a state of full awareness in the present moment. The aim of meditation is to reach a deeper level of inner consciousness.

Types of Meditation

Again, it is a case of finding what works for you. Some people find guided visualisation or meditation very effective while others find it off-putting to have someone talking to them. Some people will meditate every day and, for others, it may be less frequent. As with all these practices, I have found that the discipline of a regular schedule maintained over a period of weeks or months has more benefit than a scatter-gun approach.

There are many forms of meditation and many techniques to help discipline, focus and still the mind. Mantras, specific objects to focus on, breathing exercises, visualisation and other practices can all be practised. What is required more than any technique is patience, forgiveness and discipline. In Annex B there are some examples of guided meditations that you might use.

Creating a Meditative State

Here, I suggest a simple practice to bring you into a meditative state:

First take a few minutes before you begin to meditate to calm your mind and body. It is very difficult to stay centred and at peace when your mind is in a whirl. Check the environment to ensure there are no distractions.

Develop your own ritual to begin your meditation. Standing or sitting, get yourself into a comfortable position. I never managed to master the traditional cross-legged, Buddha-style position and will either sit on a chair with my feet on the ground or on a large cushion with my legs crossed.

Bring your attention into your physical body. As other thoughts come into your mind, just notice them but pay them no attention. Keep your focus on the body.

Feel your feet on the ground. Feel the pressure of your legs on the chair or the ground. Notice the touch of the air on your fingers. Check that your spine is straight and then relax your shoulders, let them sink with each breath towards the ground. Check that your head is not too far back, not too far forward – nestling gently, as if suspended from above by a golden cord running down your spine to the earth beneath you.

Now, bring your focus to your breath and begin to follow each breath as it flows in through your nose, down through your body to the base of your spine. Then, as it flows back out, imagine that it carries any anxiety, any concerns that you have. Slow your breath down, letting go of any other thoughts that come into your mind, feeling a sense of peace flowing in, around and through you.

From this point, you might simply stay focused on your breath – a mindful breathing practice. You might use a visualisation to take you to a deeper state, you might use colour to heal or energise. You might experiment by bringing your focus, breathing into, different parts of your body - perhaps the seven chakras - and notice any thoughts, feelings or sensations that arise. The important things in meditation are to remain focused, to remain calm and let go of any expectations or desire for something specific to happen.

It is important to close down your energy after a meditation. You become open during this activity and need to protect yourself from the negative energies that exist in the world around us. To close down, I have my own ritual - imagining each of my chakras or energy centres as a flower and gently closing the petals, starting at the crown and finishing at the base of the spine. Then I imagine drawing a golden light close around my body, like a golden cloak. Then I say thank you to those spirits close to me for their love and support and say, 'Please, close me down.'

I suggest that you use the learning journal to capture your meditation experiences, certainly in the early days to capture the lessson and insights.

Practice Small Acts of Kindness

Find a way, however small, to serve others. It may be volunteering for a charity or some other form of community and environmental work. Whatever work we do can have a higher purpose. Using our talents to serve something greater than ourselves, this has always held a spiritual quality. Stephen Covey calls it 'Living the Law of Love'.

I introduced that concept, Living the Law of Love, to groups of managers I worked with in a waste management company. These were managers of the street sweepers and the rubbish collection, so I always introduced this idea on day two, when they had had a chance to get to know me. I remember how quickly they recognised the value of this kind of servant leadership and how many of them were already doing things which reflected this law. One of the managers related how he would always carry a flask of tea and a packet of chocolate biscuits in has car as he drove around his 'patch'. Whenever he stopped to check up on the lorries or visited a site, he would always pull out the flask and hand out the mugs. It was his way of showing that he cared about his 'troops'.

There are many opportunities in the world to help others or to join others in voluntary work. Any form of self-sacrifice for the benefit of others draws on and builds the energy of our heart. It is love.

Practise Acts of Gratitude

I first met Jean d'Amour at a dinner in Cambridge. He saw that my charity was called Small Acts of Kindness and he felt compelled to come and sit next to me. His charity is called Acts of Gratitude. Jean was seven years old when he lost his entire family, except an aunt, in the Rwandan genocide. His response has been to show gratitude for what he has been given rather than to focus on what others have taken away, to create a charity, supporting and helping others. His work, his approach to life, lifts my spirit. Take time, each day, to reflect on all that we are grateful for.

Go on a Retreat (a Longer Time in the 4th Space), a Pilgrimage or Labyrinth Walk. These are different forms of symbolic journeying to a centre or to your own centre. Stepping off the path to reflect on your journey and connect with the higher dimensions.

Express Your Creativity. Painting, sculpting, writing poetry, dancing – all are ways of expressing the deepest part of you, beyond logic and intellect. Create your own symbology – like the rituals we have in our lives, symbols bring the spiritual into life. We may wear a cross around our neck, a ring on our finger or have some picture, a

crystal or an artefact on our desk. I like to keep pictures and posters around my walls to remind me of aspects of my chosen path. The wonderful Desiderata, reminds me always – 'do not compare yourself with others or you will become vain or bitter.' The more we have, the more we stay mindful of the path we have chosen.

I have found that writing poetry has helped me through some difficult times, enabling me to express something of what is happening inside. Painting too, and the use of colour to heal and to express myself, has been therapeutic as well as bringing much enjoyment.

Desiderata

Go placidly amid the noise and haste, and remember what peace there may be in silence.
As far as possible, without surrender, be on good terms with all persons.
Speak your truth quietly and clearly; and listen to others, even to the dull and ignorant; they too have their story.
Avoid loud and aggressive persons; they are vexations to the spirit.
If you compare yourself with others, you may become vain or bitter, for always there will be greater and lesser persons than yourself.
Enjoy your achievements as well as your plans.
Keep interested in your own career, however humble; it's a real possession in the changing fortunes of time.
Exercise caution in your business affairs, for the world is full of trickery. But let this not blind you to what virtue there is; many persons strive for high ideals, and everywhere life is full of heroism.
Be yourself. Especially do not feign affection. Neither be cynical about love; for in the face of all aridity and

---

> *disenchantment, it is as perennial as the grass.*
> *Take kindly the counsel of the years, gracefully*
> *surrendering the things of youth. Nurture strength of*
> *spirit to shield you in sudden misfortune. But do not*
> *distress yourself with dark imaginings. Many fears are*
> *born of fatigue and loneliness.*
> *Beyond a wholesome discipline, be gentle with yourself.*
> *You are a child of the universe no less than the trees and*
> *the stars; you have a right to be here. And whether or not*
> *it is clear to you, no doubt the universe is unfolding as it*
> *should.*
> *Therefore, be at peace with God, whatever you conceive*
> *him to be.*
> *And whatever your labours and aspirations, in the noisy*
> *confusion of life, keep peace in your soul.*
> *With all its sham, drudgery and broken dreams, it is still*
> *a beautiful world.*
> *Be cheerful. Strive to be happy.*
>
> MAX EHRMANN, 1927

Join a Spiritual Community. Although I have stressed the importance of following your own path, we are also part of something much more and there are many benefits from being part of the wider spiritual community. We can learn from others, we can encourage and be encouraged, we can help provide discipline and receive that same support for ourselves.

I still enjoy the occasional visit to a church, partly for the atmosphere of the building, but also to feel the sense of community that invariably exists in the regular congregation. I also enjoy being part of a small group from my university spiritual programme. We are all very different in so many ways and yet, together, we create a safe space to share our experiences.

Study the Mountain. Read the sacred texts or attend workshops and conferences. We walk our own path, but that does not preclude our openness to learning from others – with their different experiences of the mountain.

Walk in Nature. Right at the beginning of the journal I expressed a concern with our disconnect from the world around us. Developing a relationship and an attunement with nature – the rhythms, the immanent spirit – has many benefits for our physical, emotional, mental and spiritual health.

First, if we have an understanding that spirit is in everything, and every living thing is a manifestation of all that is, then we can come close to that spirit when we walk in nature. As a spiritual practice, a walk in the woods or sitting beside the ocean makes far more sense to me than sitting in a great stone building.

Making it Happen

'Between the theory and reality, lies the shadow'

ACTION PLANNING

This planning process comes from my experience in the army. I consider this to be one of the most powerful disciplines that I took away from those days. The same process is used for a small task and a major operation, differing only in the depth and breadth of the planning process. The thoughtfulness that it encourages saves time, lives and makes it much more likely that a goal will be achieved. I know that for many people the idea of planning is a purgatory. For many more it is quite simply a waste of time, as we know that the world will change faster than we can possibly plan for it.

I have sympathy with both those views. The American General Eisenhower once said 'Plans are useless.' In my experience, the American military like to plan everything to the minutest detail, so perhaps we shouldn't listen to him. He did, however, go on to say, 'Planning is everything.' We accept that life is constantly changing and that, to use another military expression, 'a plan never survives the first contact of battle,' but we can still remain agile, adaptive and prepared to meet those changing circumstances.

Learning or knowing the right words and the right actions is the easy bit. Saying them or doing it at the right time and in the right place, putting the lessons into practice - that is the only real measure of development. To walk this path will involve change and our nature tends to prevent change - fear, uncertainty and also comfort with 'the way that we know.'

Developing Self-Reliance

On other paths, there will be a teacher or master to remind you of your duties, your responsibilities and commitments. Even then, when we are out of the classroom, the church or the mosque, it is too easy to be distracted or to choose an easier route. I think it is a part of our nature. Next time you are in a gym, watch how people will take a rest from the exercise - especially when they know the instructor isn't looking. I've done that - and I've also chastised countless girls, boys, soldiers, men and women over the years for their lack of will or discipline

Forming the plan is a vital part of the journey. It doesn't guarantee success but even just the act of putting your ideas into words makes them more likely to happen - sharing those plans with another person increase the likelihood further. That is both from my own experience and evidence gathered over may years at Yale University in America.

Discipline in the Spiritual Life

Regardless of our personality, if we want to develop a new habit, that takes discipline and repeated practice. In Tai Chi, there is a saying that, if we wish to develop a new skill or posture, we must hold it in the front of our mind for 100 days. That's about three months! Malcolm Gladwell and Matthew Syed, who have both written about mastery or greatness, talk about the need for 10,000 hours of practice to achieve it. So, there is a need for balance - openness and discipline.

Without a clear plan and goals, things may happen ... but experience tells me that it won't. How many New Year's resolutions last beyond the first week in January? An Action Plan - and a commitment to see it through - is essential for lasting effect. So, throughout the journal, we have been leading towards the development of a plan that will take you on that upward path.

116

Statement of Intent

At the beginning of each new project, write a personal statement of intent to do all you can to move towards it. What you are committing to – why are you taking these steps? It will give a sense of how committed you are to making the changes.

THE PLANNING MODEL

Situation – the 'big picture' gives the context and describes why this project or task is important, and the impact it will have. It will describe how it fits with other projects.

Aim – this is the most important part of the plan. In the army, when a plan was being communicated, the aim was always stated twice. The details of a plan will invariably change but knowing the goal and why it is important enables the direction and momentum to be maintained. The aim contains the 'what', or the goal to be achieved. It contains the 'why', or the reason why this is important. It contains the 'how', or a statement of how the goal will be achieved and, finally, the time by which the aim will be achieved.

The Overview

Some projects and plans will contain a number of threads or projects. This part of the plan shows the priorities, a 'picture' of how the plan will unfold and how the small steps all lead to the final, destination.

Individual Goals and Tasks

This is the detailed part of the plan, which enables you to know – for each step:

- What I am doing, what resources I have (people, time, money, equipment) and how I am progressing.
- How I am going to do it.
- Why I am doing this.
- What support I have and how the plan will be co-ordinated.

The Schedule – Time and Targets

Without this schedule, things tend to drift, and it is also very difficult to measure performance – and celebrate the improvements. But they need to be realistic too. In the coaching world, there are many models of goal-setting to make them more effective. Perhaps the simplest and easiest to remember is the SMART pneumonic.

Making your goals Specific and Measurable helps motivation – rather than some vague wish or hope. The A is for Achievable and reinforces my view that you need to have realistic expectations. However, there is another model which talks about setting courageous or challenging goals, and this can also add tremendously to the level of motivation. The real challenge is to get the balance right. Then the R is for Relevant – and you should see clearly how your goal will help you to achieve the higher purpose. Finally, the T is for Time-bound and even with this spiritual journey it is a good idea to have milestones and checkpoints along the way to help motivation and development.

Testing the Plan

After you have had a chance to reflect, we need to test the plan – for clarity, realism, relevance and how compelling it is.

ANTICIPATING THE JOURNEY

There is a very predictable, premature end to this great journey of transformation. I feel inspired as I set out towards the great vision of the future that I have created. I return to my life and work full of vigour and good intention, full of what is called 'naïve enthusiasm'. All goes well for the first few days or even weeks but then, at some stage, I will face what is called 'the rude awakening'. Things will go wrong. I will make mistakes or lose motivation. Then, if I am not prepared or strong enough, I lose heart and give up. It might be a New Year's resolution or a new diet; I have experienced this story, many times.

Presenting the benefits of the vision without describing the hurdles and pitfalls on the way is dangerous. There is a real risk of shock and loss of will when the inevitable failures or setbacks occur. And so, on the journey of personal mastery you need to anticipate the roller coaster of emotions that can be waiting. If you are mentally prepared for the highs and the lows, then you will be in a much stronger position to deal with them.

At certain times on the path you may be:

Confused, disappointed by early failures, exhausted, stressed, demoralised, angry, lacking commitment, insecure, depressed, unloved and alone.

Excited and pleased with yourself, wanting recognition, wanting thanks, wanting to celebrate.

If you can anticipate these feelings, what might cause them and what is needed at that moment - at the rude awakening - then you can plan how to deal with them, in that moment.

You can put support mechanisms in place to remind you or

encourage your failing morale. You can seek a mentor or guide to share your stories and help you through the dark times.

Don't Quit

When things go wrong, as they sometimes will
When the road you're trudging seems all uphill
When the funds are low and the debts are high
And you want to smile but have to sigh;
When care is pressing you down a bit –
Rest if you must, but don't you quit.
Success is failure turned inside out
The silver glint of the clouds of doubt
And you can never tell how close you are
It may be near when it seems afar.
So, stick to the fight when you're hardest hit –
It's when things go wrong that you mustn't quit.

- AUTHOR UNKNOWN –

TRAVEL SAFELY, TRAVEL WELL

We have looked at the mountain and the great challenge it presents us. I hope that you have a sense of 'the gold within' and the benefits of shedding the mud that has covered it. Now comes the real work, to follow your own path. In the annexes that follow, there are further resources for you to draw on, gathered on my journey.

All my life, even in the solitary moments, I have never felt alone. I have always felt guided and connected to souls and a life force around me. Some of those souls have been in this world, others live in the higher dimensions. This is a paradox that I will leave you with; the path of the mystic is a challenge that we face on our own and yet, we are never alone. Perhaps that is why I loved reading this channelled prophecy.

The Church Of Love

The last of the Cathars was burnt by the Inquisition of the Roman Catholic Church at Montsegur, Languedoc, France in 1244, but they left this prophecy; that the Church of Love would be proclaimed in 1986.

It has no fabric, only understanding.
It has no membership, save those who know they belong.
It has no rivals, because it is non-competitive.
It has no ambition, it seeks only to serve.
It knows no boundaries for nationalism is unloving.
It is not of itself because it seeks to enrich all groups and religions.
It acknowledges all great teachers of all the ages who have shown the truth of love.
Those who participate, practice the truth of love in all their beings.
There is no walk of life or nationality that is a barrier.
Those who are, know.
It seeks not to teach but be and, by being, enrich.
It recognises that the way we are may be the way of those around us because we are the way.
It recognises the whole planet as a Being of which we are part.
It recognises that the time has come for the supreme transmutation, the ultimate alchemic act for conscious change of the ego into a voluntary return to the whole.
It does not proclaim itself with a loud voice but in the subtle realms of loving.

It salutes all those in the past that blazed the path but have paid the price.

It admits no hierarchy or structure, for no one is greater than the other.

Its members shall know each other by their deeds and being, and by their eyes and by no other outward sign save the fraternal embrace.

Each one will dedicate their life to the silent loving of their neighbour and environment and the planet, while carrying out their task however exalted or humble.

It recognises the supremacy of the great idea, which may only be accomplished if the human race practises the supremacy of love.

It has no reward to offer here or in the hereafter save that ineffable joy of being and loving.

Each shall seek to advance the cause of understanding, doing good by stealth and teaching and by example.

They shall heal their neighbour, their community and the Planet.

They shall feel no fear and feel no shame and their witness shall prevail over all odds.

It has no secret, no arcanum, no initiation save of the true understanding of the power of love and that, if we want it to be so, the world will change but only if we change ourselves first.

So, look for the guides on the mountain and offer support to your fellow travellers when they seek it. I offer you my blessing and my support as you set out on your hero's journey. Travel safely, travel well.

Annex A

In this annex, I will share my own philosophy with the principles and practices that support it. It has evolved over the last 25 years; the sources are my own experience and the variety of sacred writing and teaching that I have encountered. It is still evolving and I think that this is an important principle to hold as we climb higher and learn from our experiences, our level of understanding will change. We need to let go of our old habits and beliefs as our perspectives change if our wisdom is to grow.

MY PHILOSOPHY AND UNDERSTANDING OF THE NATURE OF THINGS

I wrote the first draft of this back in 2002 just before I started my postgraduate programme at the University of Surrey. I was coming to the end of my time at White Lodge and I wanted to capture my thoughts and experience. It has evolved over the years and I still consider it a draft. Each year, I reflect on and adjust it.

You will see that I have drawn from many paths and traditions but sought to create a philosophy in my own words and as an expression of me and my unique, lived experience. Here it is:

I follow no religious creed. I avoid labels and remain a free spirit in search of the truth; enabling and encouraging others to express the spiritual impulse in a way that is right for them. Freedom is at the heart of my philosophy, of my life and of me. I seek to avoid any restricting beliefs and remain as open as possible to new and deeper levels of understanding; to walk on the mountain and learn the ways of the mountain but not be tied to any single path. I enjoy learning from those paths but I follow my own inner compass, the sense of rightness, the voice of my soul.

I see spirit in everything. It feels as though it is written in my nature, although I acknowledge the danger, in that feeling, of becoming too fixed in my thinking. I have been influenced strongly by the teachings of Ronald Beesley (spiritual psychotherapy), which encompass the principles that underpin many traditions. I have a strong sense of connection to the ancient traditions – Egypt, the Vedas and Native Americans, the Tao Te Ching and Buddhism – with their many expressions of the divine presence, the spiritual impulse. Most recently I have enjoyed discovering and exploring the Toltec tradition and I will continue to explore the mountain.

Those principles are very strong within me; principles that I think and feel, through teachings, observation and my own experience, are universal in nature. As I travel in the world and through this life, I understand more of the many dimensions of humanity; our instinctive nature, our emotions, our intellect and the spiritual impulse. That knowledge has to be learnt, not just taught, felt, not just theorised. Unthinking obedience to a religion does not necessarily lead to a spiritual nature. In the same way, a person may not conform to any creed or doctrine and yet may have a strong sense of spirituality. So, as well as having a philosophy, there needs to be an active expression of that philosophy in everyday life. It may include the ritual and specific times of 'devotion' but these are in addition to our normal life pattern. What matters are the choices we take in each living moment, in how we interact with the world around us. The beauty and simplicity of the Law of Ma'at and the Eightfold Path resonate ever more strongly.

I acknowledge and embrace the concept of a divine aspect of humanity. The great world religions all hold this message and a creed that attempt to lead us to the discovery or realisation of that divinity. Love and compassion may be part of that creed but it is not the only path that people will follow in their search for the truth. There must also be, for me, the sense that this way of living enables us to evolve as a soul – to fully express our talents and fulfil our life purpose. This, in turn, leads to the evolution of humanity and the cosmos. This is the purpose of life.

THE PRINCIPLES OF MY PHILOSOPHY

These are the principles which I use to determine my personal path and the activities that will help me to walk it. You will see many links to the ancient teachings.

The Source – Unity

The first principle is that there is a universal consciousness of which we are all a part. This is the Tao of Lao Tzu, the endless flow of the cosmos. A Oneness. I do not like to use the term 'God' to describe this – it carries too much baggage; I do not feel tied to any name. Neil Donald Walsch, the author of *Conversations with God*, suggests that we might call it 'life'. This consciousness is within all things and we are all part of that whole. In the Vedic traditions, this is the concept of Atman in Brahman and Brahman in Atman. It is such an important concept in my work and the idea of service which springs from it – we are all one. It gives great meaning and importance to the role of leadership and teaching in serving others. Each of the other principles has a twin aspect, a shadow or opposite pole. Here, though, there is only the whole.

Duality – Love

The second principle is that we live in a universe of duality, of light and darkness. Light alone is incomplete; love is the binding force which connects the seeds of light together to bring form – 'ten thousand things' and all the shades of colour, a spectrum of experience. The move from oneness to separateness and back to oneness brings duality. It brings love and hate, greed and selflessness, and all thought and emotion. Like the Tai Chi symbol, there is a small element of Yin in the Yang and vice versa. It is not a linear spectrum but a continuum with no absolute, no end and no beginning. We cannot experience joy without sadness, there cannot be a thing without nothing. The shadow of love and connectedness is separation, isolation and hatred born of fear.

Evolution – the Creative Process, Life

The third principle is that the cosmos, all that is, is evolving for some reason that I do not understand – driven by a creative impulse, the life force. It cannot stop evolving, it is a constant, creative process which, by the nature of all things, involves new expressions of spirit in life, shapes and forms emerging from the old lives, shapes and forms as they decay and die. This is the cycle of life and it is written into our nature and all nature. The opposite or shadow of creation and life is destruction and death.

Responsibility, Duty, Service – Our Work

The fourth principle is that we have a responsibility for our own self and to the whole. The first responsibility is to our own higher self, beyond this physical form – to live each life to the full in order to develop our own soul. The second responsibility is to contribute to the whole; that may be to family, community or through service to a noble cause. This is our work; an expression of our talents in

126

service. We are all at differing stages of development and consciousness on the path of evolution. Right and wrong, good and bad are perceptions that change as we grow in our understanding. We learn through experience, through the lessons of life. I see my work as teaching, to guide others on their path. The opposite or shadow to responsibility and service is greed and selfishness.

Peace – Movement and Change

The fifth principle is peace. I see peace as a swirling, interwoven system of energy working in perfect harmony. Evolution involves constant change and movement; that brings conflict. Peace is not the absence of conflict; it is the presence of the means to deal with that conflict - within ourselves and between each other. Each element is vibrating to its own note and each system working within a greater system. This principle is reflected in our daily lives – with the many interacting worlds that we inhabit, the many cultures and interwoven relationships. We are learning more and more about these systems and how, through that understanding, we can live in harmony with, rather than in conflict with, the energy systems around us. This leads on to the idea of all being as it should be. The systems have an intelligence of their own, there is no 'right or wrong' in this sense and each system will restore its own pattern. My role is to bring meaning and understanding - both to initiate change and restore harmony - to bring peace of body, mind, heart and spirit. The shadow or peace is resistance, inertia and violence.

Hierarchy – Structure and Social Order

The sixth principle. I am more than open to the idea that there are many dimensions in this cosmos and within myself. I see hierarchy all around me: a natural part of existence as I know and understand it. My own understanding is deepening through experience but also the teachings of those that I trust and consider to be more evolved in consciousness than me. I am happy to accept that we can develop the faculties to reach these higher worlds and to work towards doing just that. The shadow of hierarchy is chaos, anarchy and the abuse of power.

Wisdom – Evolving Consciousness

The seventh principle: the knowledge that I seek lies within me already. Each spiritual psychotherapy course was like a revision course rather than a teaching programme. In our genes we carry physical messages, but there are other dimensional stores of knowledge waiting for us too. The challenge now is discernment – to test the vast array of knowledge, opinion and belief against an objective 'compass'. To make choices that fit with my own sense of 'rightness' I have a growing sense of authority now, of choosing wisely from feedback from others and my own self-observation of my own thoughts, words and actions. This is the purpose of life for me, to evolve to higher levels of consciousness and inspire, enable and encourage others on the same path. The shadow is hubris.

Power – the Challenge

Eighth, Atman in Brahman and Brahman in Atman. The God within us, the creative impulse within us, the ability to express our free will and to influence our own life and the lives of others. Each of us has different opportunities to experience this power; to control and to be controlled. It is a power that impacts on our instinctive, emotional and intellectual nature and the right application of this power within the world is the greatest challenge we face. It is the potential within us for greatness and the source of all abuse and violence in the world.

As I have mentioned before, I am still working on this. I know that I should find a way to link my third and seventh and sixth and eighth principles but, for now, I am happy to sit with the imperfections.

Somewhere, too, I need to capture the importance of humility, of remaining open to further insight and enlightenment. Labels and fixed beliefs lead to a closed mind, to fear and hatred. So, my philosophy remains a 'work in progress'.

MY PURPOSE AND PERSONAL PATH

So, how do all these principles impact on me and the way that I live my life? Here I have taken some elements from my own journal.

My Purpose and Guiding Principles

Heal the Body, Open the Mind, Touch the Heart, Awaken the Soul, Release the Spirit.

... My role is to hold and radiate the divine light that will awaken the soul of humanity, pierce the clouds and shadows and lift mankind to new levels of consciousness. Through teaching, coaching and embodying the principles of Truth, Peace, Light and Love within the business community and wider social fabric.

Do not be distracted by or into areas that are beyond your area of influence. Although all is interconnected and the ripples of your work will travel further than you imagine or know. Your aim is not to deal with the symptoms of our diseased society but the cause. It is our attitude and our deepest sense of purpose and intention that we seek to change ...

Light & Unity – Reverence for all Life

The first is to create a sense of deep respect and reverence for all life. Everything is an expression of light and love, of the Creative Source. It is difficult - not with the animal, acting purely from instinct, but with humans certainly - to follow this principle when the instinct and emotion scream for contrary action: that is hard.

Love (Kindness)

The second is the way of expressing the reverence for all life. My feeling is that by letting this force dictate words and actions, I will be able to live in harmony rather than conflict. It has led me to try to develop patience, forgiveness, compassion and understanding. It feels right to do so - despite a strong competitive and survival instinct.

Creativity

The third is a move to action and experience. To express the creative impulse in all areas of my life. To write, to paint, to enable learning experiences for myself and others.

My Work – Teaching

The fourth is a sense of responsibility for teaching others. Awakening the knowledge that lies within us. This is a vocation for me, and I must maintain the balance (teaching and not preaching) but working more to teach what and who I am.

Peace – Through Ma'at

The fifth is the application of the Law of Ma'at and a 'sense of rightness' in controlling and guiding my actions and words. Through mindfulness and the 4th Space I am bringing this more and more into my own work and life; first peace within, and then more and more bringing peace in the outer world through relationships and education. This area remains a challenge for me – the instinct to fight battling with a gentle and compassionate nature. Mindfulness is helping me to hold the tension and balance.

Humility and Honour

The **sixth** is an acknowledgement of my place in the great circle of life. It is to honour my ancestors, my parents and my teachers – all of them. It is acknowledging with joy the blessings I have received and use them in service. It leads to the support of those who follow and to seek and accept the support from those who are on higher levels.

Seek and Ye Shall Find

The seventh is to search for wisdom – to seek to awaken my knowledge, understanding and the faculties that will enable me to access the higher worlds.

Power

The eighth is the personal quest for mastery of my own nature through awareness and understanding. Second, it is through my leadership work, developing the awareness and understanding in all those with whom I work to use their power in a right way. Perhaps this is my most important work – until we humans learn to deal with this part of us, then our world, as we know it, seems doomed. The warrior is a strong voice within me and I feed it with my physical fitness.

Now, I was ready to create my own personal code – my statement of intent, my compass to keep me heading in the right direction on the mountain. You will see that I have called it the Gentle Warrior.

This has a special meaning to me reflected in the two symbols I chose to represent my code. The sword is the symbol, to me, of strength and the warrior. The chalice is the symbol, to me, of the Divine Feminine and of love. They represent my quest to hold the balance, to be the gentle warrior.

THE GENTLE WARRIOR – MY CODE

My code embodies, for me, the purpose of my life in this world: the fulfilment of my own soul's purpose to serve the greater cause of human and cosmic evolution. It is the quest for perfection in an imperfect world. This is my own code, my choice. It is not imposed – although I have learnt from the paths that others have broken for me.

To follow this path, I need commitment, courage and discipline. In the army and on the sports field I trained hard, but after the session, operation or the game I could rest. On this path, where the result will not be known in this lifetime and where every waking moment is 'an event', it is a constant challenge to maintain the levels of performance that I expect of myself.

Reverence for All Life. I will treat all life and all manifestations of the Divine Spirit as sacred. However hard this may be - not so much with the mosquitoes and midges (although that is tough), but with the selfish and violent behaviours of mankind.

Heart and Soul. I will work to express my soul purpose in all that I do. Heal the body, open the mind, touch the heart, awaken the soul and release the spirit of humanity. Be all that I can be and do all that I can do.

Be the Change. Actions not words. Actions not intentions. My work is my life and my life is my work

Service. My duty is to serve – others and this path. I will use my talents to teach, heal, protect, support and help those who need help to walk towards the light – if they are ready.

Ma'at. I will honour and live in accordance with what was known by the Ancient Egyptians as the Law of Ma'at and by the Buddhists as the Eightfold Path. I will seek a sense of 'rightness' in all I think, say and do. In an imperfect world, a world of duality, I will fight for peace, strive for harmony and seek to bring light to the darkness.

Honour and Humility. I honour my ancestors and my children, tradition and freedom, my teachers and my own wisdom. I will impose on nobody but I will stand against those who do. I accept responsibility for my own path. I will nurture humility.

Personal Mastery. I will live mindfully and always seek to be guided in thought, word and action by the quiet voice of my soul. To choose the path of love. I will search endlessly for the Truth that lies within and develop a mastery of my physical, mental, emotional and spiritual bodies by striving for peace within myself and seeking to be a peacemaker in my daily life; by accepting suffering rather than inflicting it; by refusing to retaliate in the face of provocation and violence; by persevering in nonviolence of tongue and heart; by living conscientiously and simply so that I do not deprive others of the means to live; by actively resisting evil and working non-violently to abolish war and the causes of war from my own heart and from the face of the Earth.

My Spiritual Practice

The spiritual impulse has been very strong within me from early childhood. It grows as I feed it. I work best alone, with a guiding framework and the flexibility to change and adapt. Yet, I know that discipline is the key to mastery and my aim is to refine my state of being, become purer in thought and deed. Maintaining my spiritual practices will provide the foundations of my work as a spiritual teacher and facilitator.

The practices listed below are taken from my latest journal. Over the years, they have changes as I have tried different practices - but not too much. Even the carrying of my journal with me, containing my philosophy and personal code is, to me, a spiritual practice. It is there as a reminder that I need to stay mindful and true to my commitments, true to the higher path.

Mindfulness

Developing mindfulness is the key to mastery. I will practise mindfulness every day. One short walking meditation, a routine daily Qi Gong practice and using Tai Chi to develop breathing and physical mindfulness. I will think - Namaste! I will dissolve bigotry within my own thinking. I will continue to keep this journal close to me - keeping my code in the front of my mind.

The Camp Fire

This is another aspect of living mindfully. Review and planning provide a celebration of my work and life but also express the discipline and desire to evolve and fully utilise my talents. I will place two dates in the diary each year to spend on this planning - one in December in mid-winter (December 28-30th) and one in mid-summer (June 21st).

Relationship with the Higher Dimensions

I have a ritual prayer each morning, making a connection with the higher dimensions. I also link to the natural world on my walks and enjoy that relationship. To help develop mindfulness I will meditate regularly daily for 20 minutes.

Kemet – Spirit in Daily Life

To remind me to adopt a spiritual approach to all life (before meetings, when responding to people etc.), I will say a short prayer before work events and use the Choka Rei symbol before events.

The Physical

My physical exercise is a spiritual practice and I will acknowledge this before each session. My vegetarian diet is a constant way to express a reverence for all life. It keeps this principle at the front of my mind. Before each meal I will acknowledge the gift of life. I already have a close connection with nature and I will continue to walk in the woods, and consciously connect with nature as part of daily routine.

Reiki

I will maintain my links to the healing world - through Kent International Healers and through Reiki. I will bring the symbols and their power more into my work.

Annex B

A Guided Meditation

The 4th Space is a time and place of stillness, of reflection and deep contemplation. Ideally, the environment will reflect that and you will be able to find a quiet space that reflects those qualities. But it is also an inner space and you need to cultivate a practice and discipline that will create the conditions for reflection and inner calm.

There are many tried and tested techniques to change our state of mind and our emotional body. Modern psychology and ancient mystical traditions provide a rich source. Later in the journal, I will talk more about mindfulness and its role on the journey of mastery. Here, I will describe a simple mindfulness practice that can quickly bring a state of inner coherence and calm.

Find a Position, sitting or lying, that is comfortable, and where you will not be too distracted by aches and pains (or fall asleep). Posture is important; try to keep the spine straight and the head centred and balanced.

Be Fully Present - bring your attention to your physical body. Notice the sensations in the different parts of your body, starting at the feet and working up to your head. Notice the sounds in and around the room.

Bring Your Attention to Your Breath. As you breathe, notice the passage of the air. Notice the movement and sensations in your body. Then focus your mind on your breathing, deep down into your body (by pushing the abdomen out). Establish a deep, slow rhythm.

Visualise Each Breath. Flowing in through the nose, down into your body, filling each part of your body - the arms, the legs, the hands, the feet - reaching into every cell. As you breathe out, picture or feel any negative feelings or thoughts flowing back out of your body - out of your nose, out of your fingers or out of your toes. You choose. Take your time over this.

Gentle Discipline. Your mind will wander. As thoughts keep appearing in your mind to distract you, gently push them away and bring your attention back to the breath. This is a discipline in itself. It gets easier with practice.

SOUL SEARCHING – WHO AM I?

A Guided Meditation

Settle yourself into a relaxed, comfortable, alert position.

Begin by bringing your awareness into your physical body. Bring your attention to your feet, where they touch the ground, where they don't touch. Be aware of other thoughts as they come into your mind but do not follow them. Notice them, acknowledge them, and gently let them go, bringing your focus back to your feet. Move your attention through your body, noticing the sensations inside your body and outside - the touch of the air or the ground on your skin.

As you are sensing the different parts of your body ask yourself,

'Who is feeling? Not the leg, not the arm. Who is conscious of these feelings? I am not this body.'

Now bring your awareness to your breath. Follow each breath in through the nose, feel the chest expand. Follow each breath back out and pause, empty, before breathing in again. Each breath is bringing life. Without it, we die. Yet each breath out, that breath has gone - we are not the breath.

Continue to focus your attention on your breath but as you do so, notice what other thoughts come into your mind. Notice how they arise from my words, notice how they might arise from feelings within you, notice how they spring from nowhere - isn't that interesting? The Buddhists talk about the chattering monkey - a hundred chattering monkeys in a single tree. Notice what thoughts come into your mind as I am speaking. So, where do these thoughts, these memories come from, and where do they go? Remember some special event in your childhood, recall the sights and the voices or sounds, relive the emotion of that moment. Who is remembering, who is watching, who is feeling? You are not your thoughts; you are the one who holds them and you are the one who lets them go. You are the one who notices.

So, who are you? Just for a moment become aware of your name, say it quietly to yourself. In your imagination, write your name on a whiteboard in front of you - and then watch the letters disappear or fly away. The letters are gone but you remain.

Just for a moment, reflect on all the roles you have played or are playing in your life. Think of yourself back when you were a child, perhaps with a brother or sister - now you have grown are you a different person, do you change with the new roles that you have now? Think of yourself as a parent, as a friend, as a colleague - each time you change role and change your behaviour, are you someone different or are the roles just roles you play? So, who are you?

Who is watching, who is experiencing? The quiet, silent watcher - the one who notices the thoughts but is not the thought, the one who experiences the feeling but is not the feeling.

You are the Atman, the seed of light. You are the ruler of this inner world, the judge, the master or mistress in your own temple. You are beyond thought, beyond feeling – you are in this body but it is not you.

So, now you listen and watch from a new place, not in the valley, blown by the winds – your thoughts and feelings governed by other people and the events of life around you.

Now you are listening as the quiet watcher within, you are higher on the mountain, perhaps even floating above it, like an eagle in the sky. You notice your feelings – your anger and your joy – but you are not governed by them. You notice your thoughts, your prejudices, your likes and your lies, but you know them for what they are.

Now, the choices you make come from your heart and soul – you choose the thoughts to follow and those to let go, you choose the feelings you adopt and you choose the way you react to the people around you.

You are your own master, you are your own God.

And now, in your imagination, the mind of your soul, you stand on the mountain. Look around you at those who travel with you on this great journey, who share this beautiful world with you. What do you see, what do you hear and what do you feel?

Can you look beyond the expression on their face, the colour of their skin? That is not their true self. Can you look beyond the way that they speak or the emotions they display? That is not their true self.

They are like you, a seed of light, a soul passing through this life, journeying on the mountain. They are from the same sun – the same source of pure light and love. We are all one.

JOURNEY TO THE CENTRE

A Guided Meditation

Enter the 4th Space using the guided meditation above.

When you are in a relaxed state and you are feeling centred and calm, move into this next stage.

Imagine yourself walking along a country path. Take a moment to notice and enjoy the sights and sounds around you. The blue sky, the many shades of green fields and trees. Imagine the warmth of the sun on your face as you walk along the path.

Imagine yourself walking off the path towards a forest. Move into the forest and take a moment to notice and enjoy the changing sights, sounds and smells. It is cooler here but the sun still shimmers through the leaves. Enjoy the stillness, broken by the sound of small animals in the undergrowth and the smell of the earth and the fallen leaves.

Imagine yourself moving through the forest towards the sound of a small stream flowing over the rocks. As you come to the stream, take some time to enjoy the sight and sound of the water tumbling over the rocks and then begin to follow a small path beside the stream down the slope. Push through the bushes at the bottom of the slope and see a beautiful lake stretching away to the mountains in the distance.

Take a moment to enjoy the sights and the stillness. The reflection of the blue sky in the mirror-like surface of the lake, bordered by the trees of the forest and the mountains. In the centre of the lake, you see a small island – a perfect emerald jewel at the heart of the lake. You feel a strong pull from the island, a need for you to be there.

Imagine then, as you stand beside the lake, you see a small boat tied to a tree. Step into the boat, untie the rope and feel the boat begin, as if drawn by a magic hand, to move out over the lake

140

towards the island. As you sit, perfectly relxed in the boat, you feel a growing sense of peace as you move from the shore and away from daily life. Take a moment to enjoy the gentle sway of the boat, the sound of the water beneath the boat.

Imagine now, as the boat reaches the island, how you climb out of the boat and walk up a grassy bank towards a small grove of ancient trees at the centre of the island. As you walk beneath the great branches you feel a deep sense of familiarity, of belonging, of being at home. As you notice the great roots of the trees you feel a deep sense of connection to the Earth, to nature. As you look up through the branches and leaves to the sun and the sky, you feel a strong sesne of connection to the heavens above you.

Beneath the largest of the great trees is a small temple, simple but beautiful, full of light, and here you feel that you have reached the very centre of your own being and the centre of all that is. You move inside and sit in silence - just for a few moments, in stillness.

After a few moments, you feel the loving presence of a great soul close to you. You know this to be your guide and teacher. Sit for a while, just being there. You may ask a question or ask for guidance, but let that question or request just sit there too. The answer may come in a way that you do not expect.

After a time of stillness in this precious space, begin to move back the way that you came, across the lake, through the forest and back into the sun. Then bring your attention into your body once again and notice the rise and fall of your chest, your feet firmly on the ground.

Gently open your eyes and enjoy the sense of peace as you come back into this other space.

DETERMINE YOUR LIFE PURPOSE

A Guided Meditation

This is a powerful question to ask yourself. Imagine that your life has a unique purpose and that you have been given this opportunity to fulfil this purpose.

That purpose is fulfilled by the way that you live your life, and will be reflected in your personal vision. It could be to perform some service for the community or to develop an aspect of yourself. It could be both.

What is that purpose? Why are you here?

One way to approach this is to go into a meditation.

Meditation on Destiny

Bring the mind into a state of calm, focused attention through breath and centring.

Imagine yourself transported far away from Earth. Look back to see our planet and then picture yourself in a different, heavenly world, entering the Great Halls of Learning where the histories of the universe are stored and studied. Here, you are relaxed and calm; you have no physical body, you are aware of yourself but also that you are part of the greater consciousness that surrounds you.

Imagine yourself approaching a doorway. You have been called to meet with the spiritual leader of this heavenly place, infinitely wise and an embodiment of light and love. It is time for you to engage in a new experience to further educate your soul.

In the presence of this great being, you are reminded of the great project that has been initiated on the planet Earth. As you sit, an image appears in front of you. A beautiful sphere of blue and green with swirling white threads, suspended in space.

Here, on this planet many souls have been given the opportunity to broaden and deepen their experience. It is a world of matter, denser than any other planet where living beings can see, hear and touch physical matter. Here they can experience a range of feelings and emotions beyond those open to you at this level.

As you sit, you feel memories stirring inside you. For you have been a part of this project before over many centuries and many lives. Each life, in different cultures, has added to your talents and wisdom. Reflect for a moment and see what memories of ancient civilisations and different lives come into your consciousness.

You become aware once again that the great challenge of evolution has always been to raise the whole of creation to new levels of consciousness. By expanding the fields of consciousness on Earth, this project was designed to greatly enhance our evolutionary path. But it has not been a smooth path.

Here it is clear to you that the density of life on Earth clouds that purpose. Our true destiny is lost amidst the distractions of these emotions and feelings, shut away by the small mind and will of the body we inhabit. There have been cycles of light and darkness - you remember that you have experienced both as you have learnt your lessons and fulfilled your own destiny. But now is a critical time - with the potential to move humanity forward further into the light and along the evolutionary path.

As you sit in the presence of this great being you become aware of past memories; that there are many people striving to find and follow their destiny. You become aware of a desire surrounding and filling you, to return to follow yours - to help create a world and a way of life that reflects our true and divine nature. There will be many distractions and the purpose must be clear and strong so that you can remain focused on it. By doing this you will serve your fellow souls and you will serve this great being.

As you sit in this space, let your deepest intuition answer these questions. As you look back on your life as a preparation for your work now, what talents do you have or have you grown? What is your true vocation; what work gives you a sense of deep fulfilment, of timelessness? What are the threats to our world and our way of life? What are you drawn to do – to make a difference? What are you on Earth for? What is your destiny?

PERSONAL VALUES

'Ultimately, it is our values that provide the stars by which we navigate through life.'

We will develop many new skills and behaviours – and that is important. But, ultimately, I see the true goal and measure of personal development as the quality of being that you are, the values that you reflect and embody. Your skills are a part of that but are like the outer skin on the onion.

This is an exercise designed to help you understand more about the values that drive you, what they mean to you and what behaviours you need to display to move towards them.

A value is an enduring belief that a certain state of being is preferable to the opposite. These are our personal views of what we find worthwhile and they come from many sources – parents, religion, school, role models and our culture. They drive our behaviour and shape our identity so we need to understand them, where they come from and whether we choose to accept and live them

Now, there will be certain values that we 'say' we believe in, or that we have been encouraged by others to hold. I want to know what springs from your heart, from your soul – they may be the

144

same as those of your parents or your upbringing but, for authenticity, integrity and the foundations of real courage, this is important to know.

If your way of life and work and your values are aligned, then you and others will have the sense of integrity from which springs respect or trust.

Preparing for Reflection

You need to find a time and space to give this exercise the appropriate level of concentration and commitment. With all these reflective exercises, some will find them easier than others. The words of St Augustine are a good reminder – you are worth this time and effort.

Testing the Values

Select your ten most important values from the list. These are the values that most affect the way that you behave or give the greatest sense of personal value and self-worth. Add your own values if you need to.

Now mark the most important five values. Test them against each other. Which one is more important to you? Then cross of the least important one until you are left with just one, the one that you care about most.

What Do They Mean in Practice?

Now, take the top three values on your list and ask yourself the following questions:

What do they mean in terms of behaviour and the way that I work and live? What do I expect from myself even in the bad times?

How well do I live these values now? What would others say?

How would life be different if these values were prominent and practised?

What would a company be like that encouraged these values? Do I work in one? If not, then what can I do to change that?

Does my personal vision (if completed) reflect these values?

Am I willing to live and work towards these values?

Values

Some of the words below are similar, but different words hold different meanings for us, so simply choose the ones that hold the quality or meaning that you wish to reflect in your work and life, and how you would like others to see you.

Achievement		Country	
Advancement		Courage	
Adventure		Creativity	
Affection		Decisiveness	
Authority		Democracy	
Autonomy		Environment	
Balance		Efficiency	
Challenge		Excellence	
Community		Excitement	
Compassion		Expertise	
Competence		Faith	
Competition		Fame	
Control		Financial gain	
Co-operation		Freedom	

Friendship		Physical challenge	
Fulfilment		Pleasure	
Growth		Power	
Family		Privacy	
Friendship		Purity	
Health and fitness		Quality	
Honesty		Relationships	
Independence		Recognition	
Influence		Religion	
Inner harmony		Reputation	
Integrity		Responsibility	
Joy		Self-respect	
Justice		Status	
Kindness		Security	
Knowledge		Service	
Love		Serenity	
Loyalty		Truth	
Meaningful work		Variety	
Nature		Wealth	
Openness		Wisdom	
Order, stability		Working with others	
Peace			

Personal Definition of Values

Select the four values that are most important to you from the list
above. What does each value mean to you? What behaviours do you
need to display to live out this value?

CREATING YOUR PERSONAL VISION

This exercise is designed to help you clarify your personal vision and path in life. The vision does not have to be some specific position or job. It is a perception of who you want to be, how you want to work and live your life. It may incorporate elements such as financial status, but this normally is a stepping stone to other qualities that you aspire to. It can also change – as we go through life our values and perspective change.

Preparation

A personal vision requires commitment. If it is to mean anything, then it will influence all your decisions and actions. So, if this is to be more than just a casual exercise, make sure that you are in the right frame of mind before you begin.

Create a time for your 4th Space, where you will not be disturbed in your thoughts or feel inhibited by others around you. Recognise that this is time being spent on your life, and value that time as a gift to yourself.

Break the Chains That Bind Us

You may experience some of the following thoughts:

Better not to raise hopes and expectations, I don't want to fail. I do not want to seem foolish in the eyes of others or go against the wishes and expectations of others. What will I have to sacrifice?

I know that in some cultures the parents choose their children's career and their partners. It seems to me that this creates a continuous cycle of people taking responsibility for someone else's life and never for their own. You may be right about the current situation but that doesn't mean that situation cannot change. In fact, if you want it to change, how will you feel in five or ten years if nothing has changed - and you have done nothing to change it? The cynics may be satisfied; they will have proved themselves right. Don't let the cynics win.

We can spend our life seeking to meet other people's expectations, living out their hopes and dreams. This is your vision. Take responsibility for your own life and how you want to live. This vision is not a static thing; it should always be just peeping over the horizon. I wrote my first vision in 1992 - for the year 2000. In 1998, I wrote my next one - for 2012, pushing the horizons a bit further. I felt the need to write again in 2010.

The idea of sacrifice can be frightening, Remember how, when I first started on my own spiritual journey, I was terrified with the idea by the expression, 'Give up all and follow me.' I know. 'What if I decide that I want to leave this job or relationship. Will I be out of control?' This is your vision and you have freedom to choose. If something is too frightening or too uncomfortable, then leave it. But if it is compelling, then you may need to come back to it when the time is right.

A vision does not need to be specific. Indeed, it is better not to be. Rather it should describe how we want to be - the kind of place we want to live and the nature of the relationships we would like to be a part of.

Creating the Vision

Imagine living where you would love to live and doing what you would love to do, both at work and outside work. What do you see, hear and feel? Take some time to 'live through a day' full of the activities that you wish for yourself. Ask yourself what it is about those activities that bring you fulfilment and joy. Take time to plan a year and how you will live or travel through each of the seasons. Imagine yourself meeting the people or the sort of people whom you wish to have relationships of any kind with.

Ignore for these few moments the 'possibility or impossibility'; imagine yourself living this life and all that this means. Be who you want to be. Dream a little.

Now describe or sketch the experience that you have just had. Use the present tense as though it is real now. There is a saying that 'If you can dream it, you can draw it. If you can draw it, you can design it. If you can design it, you can do it.'

Defining the Vision

Through your visioning you have imagined a state of fulfilment. You have created a world for yourself where you are all that you wish to be, self-actualised.

To give some form to that feeling, draw out the answers to some, or all, of the following questions from your visioning exercise:

- **Self-image** – describe the qualities and values that you wish to see reflected in yourself. How do you see yourself physically, emotionally, intellectually and spiritually?
- **Material** – what material things do you want around you? Look around you and see what you want to see. Is it a simple, uncluttered life with few possessions or full of high-quality furnishings?
- **Home** – where do you live? What kind of home do you have? What environment do you live in? Is there are garden, and if so how big and what features do you have in it? Is there a view from your bedroom window?
- **Health** – what state of fitness do you have, what do you eat and drink, what sports do you play, how do you look after yourself?
- **Relationships** – what type of relationships do you have with

family, friends, colleagues and others? How often to do you meet and what do you do together? What do your friends and family say about you? How would they describe you?

- **Work** – what do you enjoy about your work? What is your ideal vocation or profession? What impact do you have in your work? What are your strengths and how do you use them? What value do you bring to your family, your community, the country, the world? Where do you work? Do you belong to a large organisation, a small company or do you work alone? How do you feel at the end of the working day?
- **Personal Development** – what personal activities do you pursue for enjoyment or for learning? What activities do you undertake to bring balance into your life on the physical, intellectual, emotional and spiritual levels? How much time do you spend on yourself in this way and where do you spend it?
- **Community** – what is your vision for the community or society that you live in? What are the values that are reflected in the way that people live? How do people interact, what do you do together? What part do you play in that vision?
- **Other Areas** – what else, in any other area of your life, would you like to create?

Clarifying your Vision

There is likely to be a mixture of selfish and selfless elements. There is no right or wrong in this, but it is important to know which parts of your vision are closest to your deepest desires – to know what you really want in life. To help clarify your vision, ask the following questions about all the elements covered above:

Why is this important to me? What will this bring me?

This question is designed to help you think through each element, both why you want it and also what is involved. For example, you may want to be a chief executive until you think of the responsibility and workload that this brings. You may settle to be a master craftsman. You may wish for a country mansion – until you think of the friends who no longer call because they think you are too 'high and mighty'. You may amend your vision to a large, welcoming home with a peaceful garden and great views.

Why is this important to me? What will this bring me?

Keep asking this until you get down to the underlying drivers for your vision. A fast, powerful car may be an important part of your vision but this question helps look beyond that and identify what it will bring you. It may be a sense of freedom, and this can then bring other ideas that will give you the same sense of freedom – a healthy body etc. Find the three or four driving forces in your life: *this is what you deeply want and can be the guiding force for your life.* It can help you to avoid getting fixed on one goal and open wider opportunities. It can help to give meaning to all that you do and all that you have done.

MINDFULNESS PRACTICES

'How long does it take – to become mindful?' That's a common question, and there is no straightforward answer. One might be 'Until you stop', as the mind will never switch off. It's like training any other part of the body: it does get easier as you go along but, as soon as you stop exercising or practising, then the muscle loses its power.

It can seem that the goal of the Body Scan or a Sitting Meditation is to stay focused on exactly one thing at a time (ankle, wrist, breath) and that when you notice your awareness has moved (to a memory, internal narrative, sound and wonderings about the sound) you are somehow failing. These practices will increase your ability to focus and concentrate, but they will also expand your ability to be with whatever comes into your field of experience, non-judgementally. *Just noticing that your attention has moved to another object is mindfulness in action.* Mindfulness includes both a concentrative attention (a laser beam) *and* a capacity to perceive a larger picture (a floodlight). Both are important. Focusing on only one thing leaves the larger picture unseen, and maintaining only a broad focus does not allow exploration of the parts.

Kabat-Zinn created an eight-week mindfulness training programme and this has become the standard format for trainers and practitioners. The important thing for those who want to walk this path is regular, daily practice and discipline. I have included some practices below. From my own experience, there is an expression in Tai Chi called the 'hundred-day rule' and it captures the idea that to embed a new habit, you need to carry the intention and practise the skill or behaviour for one hundred days.

The Skills

- Knowing that your attention is not where you want it to be.
- Unhooking your attention from that unwanted place.
- Consciously placing your attention where you do want it to be.
- Keeping your attention where you want it to be.

Daily Practices?

The Body Scan Meditation – 20 minutes

Lay down so mewhere comfortable and where you will not be disturbed.

Bring your attention into your body. Become aware and pay attention to the physical sensations - where you touch the ground or bed, to the movement of your body as you breathe. On each breath out sink a little deeper into the floor or bed.

Remember quietly that the aim is to be fully awake. It is not to feel anything - just to bring your attention to the sensations in the body and move your focus around the body.

Bring you attention to the Tan Tien. Feel the sensations in the abdomen as you breathe in and out.

Now move your focus to the left leg. Begin at the toes and spend time noticing the sensations in the toes, the foot, the calf, the knee, the thigh, and the hip. No right or wrong, just be curious.

Now focus on the breath and breathe down through the left leg to the toes. Spend time breathing into each part of the left leg. Then move to the right leg and repeat. Then move to the groin, genitals, buttocks, hips, chest, fingers, hands, arms, shoulders, jaw, nose and eyes. Forehead and crown.

When you become aware of any tension or other sensations, breathe into them and maintain the curiosity - pay attention to the way the sensation feels, how it moves or changes.

Each time your thoughts wander and you notice, gently bring

your attention back to the body and the breath. If you find yourself falling asleep, change your posture to remain alert and awake.

If your mind wanders a lot, notice the thoughts as passing events and bring your attention gently back. There is no success or failure – this is not something you can do right or wrong. Be open and curious. Let go of any expectations; do not strive to feel anything or to feel successful.

Breathing Meditation – 10 minutes

Sit comfortably, back straight and feet flat on floor. Eyes gently closed or unfocused. Bring your attention into your body. Become aware and pay attention to the physical sensations – pressure of feet on the floor, contact with the seat, the set of your shoulders (and relax them), the position of your chin (slightly tucked in). Spend a minute or two being present in this way, noticing the sensations.

Follow the breath. Bring your attention to the breath – just notice, no need to do anything. Follow the sensations for the full breath and notice any pauses in the breathing rhythm. Do not try to control the breath, simply let it flow. You are not trying to achieve a particular state, simply accept your experience as your experience. Just notice. Notice the sensations that come with each breath – the air through the nose, the rise and fall of the chest or abdomen.

Bring the mind back. Your mind will wander. When it does, notice where it has gone and bring it gently back to the breath. Notice any self-criticism or judgement, acknowledge it and gently return to non-judgemental awareness. Each time you notice the mind wandering and bring it back, it is a small step and triumph on the journey of mastery.

If your mind wanders a lot, notice the thoughts as passing events and bring your attention gently back. There is no success or failure – this is not something you can do right or wrong. Be open and curious. Let go of any expectations; do not strive to feel anything or to feel successful.

Mindful Walking

Find a place where you can walk up and down without concerns of people watching you.

Stand at the start of the walking lane, feet parallel, knees slightly bent, arms loose by your side, back straight, eyes gently focused ahead.

Bring your attention to the bottom of your feet, feel the contact with the ground. Feel the sensations in your legs, holding the weight, holding the balance, the flow of energy.

Allow the left heel to rise from the ground as you begin to take a pace. Slowly. Give yourself time to experience the different sensations in your body - the calf muscle, the whole leg as you move it forward to rest your left heel on the ground. Pay attention to the sensations in your right leg as it takes your full weight and the balance shifts. Bring your whole attention to the left foot as it touches the ground attention.

Now the right heel rises and you shift your full attention to the sensations in you right leg. And the pattern is repeated as you take the next step.

When you reach the end of the lane, turn slowly, appreciating the incredible complex series of thoughts and movements that are involved.

Keep walking, and as your thoughts wander, as they will, bring them back to the physical actions within the body. Reconnect with the physical sensations.

Practise for 15 minutes, slowing down and speeding up but maintaining the attention and focus. Perhaps if you feel agitated you might speed up, but then see if slowing down calms the mind too.

You can bring this practice into your everyday walking.

Mindful Relationships

When you are with others, consciously bring your attention to your physical body as you listen to them. Pay attention to physical sensations, thoughts, feelings and any reactions.

Pay full attention to the words, facial expressions and body position of the other person. Notice the sensations that may arise as a result of them.

Mindful Eating

Take time to centre yourself before eating. Bring your attention fully into the present, into the physical body.

Take time to notice the incredible complexity of thought and physical movement in each action; the lifting of the fork, the movement of the food to the mouth, the chewing, the swallowing.

Take time to chew slowly and notice the sensations within the mouth, the throat, and the stomach as you take the first bite, then the second. Take time to notice if the sensations change as you continue eating.

The Set-up. Find a quiet space and a time (10–15 mins) where you can sit uninterrupted and unobserved. Settle yourself and give your full attention to this practice.

Touching, Observing – be aware of the weight of the food, notice the colour, shape, texture.

Feeling – as you raise the food to your mouth, be conscious of movement in your muscles. If you are eating with your hands (recommended) notice the feel of the food, the texture, the softness.

Sensations – throughout the exercise as you move between sight, smell, touch notice any inner sensations, in your mouth, in your stomach.

Sight and smell – lift the food close and notice the detail that you can see, the minute details. As you lift the food to your mouth notice any fragrance – breath in over the food a few times.

Placing – bring the food to your lips and touch – notice the delicate sensation. Place it on your tongue – let it rest there. Don't chew. Notice any sensations.

Taste - take a single bite, don't chew. What do you notice, what do you taste? Take another, single bite. What do you notice? Any difference?

Chewing - very slowly. Don't swallow. Keep chewing until there is almost nothing left then ...

Swallow - and notice the intention.

Finish - follow the path of food until you lose it. What do you notice now - feelings, awareness? What have you become aware of through this exercise?

Staying Present - 2–3 minutes

Use your body as a way of staying fully present. Stay mindful of your posture and be aware of the sensations in your body, right now. Be 'in' your body as you sit, stand, turn, walk, wash.

This is so simple. Practise bringing your attention back to your physical body - again and again. In this way, you begin to live mindfully in the world.

The Breathing Space - Centreing Exercise - 2–3 minutes

Consciously bring yourself into the present moment, right here, right now, by bringing your attention into your physical body.

Ground yourself - sitting or standing. Straighten your back, sitting or standing, so that you have an upright, dignified posture allowing the energy to flow freely. Pull the shoulders back and then relax them, let them drop. The head nestling gently, as if suspended from above by a golden cord.

Notice the thoughts, feelings and physical sensations. Maintain an attitude of curiosity. Move to explore the sensation and perhaps describe it.

Bring your attention to your breathing. You may count as you breathe in and out, noticing the pauses. Notice the sensations as you breathe in and out. As your thoughts wander, gently keep bringing them back to the rhythm of the breath.

Expand your attention. Notice the sounds near and far, but acknowledge that they are just sounds, bring your attention back to the breath.

Expand your attention to the whole body, noticing, acknowledging and accepting any discomfort, tensions. Breathe into them and breathe them out.

Expand your mindfulness to connect these moments of full 'awareness' into the next moments of your life.

Appreciative Moments

Pay attention to how you experience and process pleasant events. They don't need to be major events; they can be something as simple as noticing the sun on your face or someone smiling at you. Just as we did last week, allow a few minutes before going to sleep to complete the journal – *writing three things that you are grateful for.*

Mindful Daily Routines

Bring your mindful awareness to some otherwise routine activity such as washing the dishes and/or eating a meal. At the end of each day, using the journal, take just five minutes to see if you can recall a daily activity which you brought awareness to that day.

Ways to Be Mindful at Work

Take 5-30 minutes in the morning to be quiet or to meditate. Gaze out of the window. Listen to the sounds of the world around you, Take a slow quiet walk.

When you sit in your car, before you turn on the engine, take a moment to connect with your breath.

In the car or train on the way home, sit quietly and make the transition from work to home.

While driving, pay full attention to the act of driving. Notice the pressure of your hands on the wheel, your posture, the movement of your hands, the movements on the road, on the pavement.

While driving, experiment by slowing down and driving just below the speed limit. What do you notice? How does that feel?

Sitting at your desk, take a moment to pay attention to your physical body, the sensations. Notice any tensions, breathe into them and let them go.

Use your breaks to consciously relax. Take a short mindful walk, breathe mindfully.

Choose to eat one or two lunches silently and mindfully.

Practice for Week 1

The Daily Practices for the Week

Day / Date	Practice	Comments

Practice for Week 2

The Daily Practices for the Week

Day / Date	Practice	Comments

Practice for Week 3

The Daily Practices for the Week

Day / Date	Practice	Comments

Practice for Week 4

The Daily Practices for the Week

Day / Date	Practice	Comments

Practice for Week 5

The Daily Practices for the Week

Day / Date	Practice	Comments

Practice for Week 6

The Daily Practices for the Week

Day / Date	Practice	Comments

Practice for Week 7

The Daily Practices for the Week

Day / Date	Practice	Comments

Practice for Week 8

The Daily Practices for the Week

Day / Date	Practice	Comments

CLEARING THE MIND

Understanding our Beliefs

We know from the study of psychology that our beliefs about ourselves influence our thoughts, and these, in turn, influence our behaviour. Our 'computer', as Stephen Peters describes the parietal brain, is incredibly fast and powerful. It is programmed from our earliest days with 'scripts' and narratives from our parents, our culture and our own experiences. Those scripts contain our unconscious prejudices and can often stop us from listening to a new idea or to a particular person or trying a new approach. They contain our own views of ourself, our capability, our potential, and can prevent us from achieving what we might otherwise achieve. It is through the challenging of this programming that the great breakthroughs in sport, business and personal achievement have occurred.

Mind–Body Link

We talk about our physique and our mental state as if they are separate. They are not. Our mental, emotional and physical states are interwoven. By changing one, we change everything. Often, though, we try to change the physical - a skill or behaviour - without touching the thought or belief that lies behind it.

We need to know and understand our beliefs and our thought processes - our programming, our attachments. Then, we make choices as to whether we change them. By changing them, we will change our performance.

| Beliefs and Scripts | → | Thoughts (Self-talk) | → | Behaviour (Performance) |

Belief Patterns

Rather than automatically thinking and behaving in a way that is consistent with our beliefs, we can choose to change those inner beliefs and thought processes and change the resulting behaviour and performance.

You may be concerned that, by changing our beliefs, we are in some way tampering with an absolute, with something unchangeable deep within us. The Earth is flat; it is impossible to run a mile in under four minutes; all 'those' people are evil - these are examples of beliefs that have held us back in the past. How foolish they seem now.

UNDERSTANDING OUR BELIEFS AND CLEARING THE MIND

The study of psychology helps us to understand the nature of the brain. There are many models and authors to give us insights.

Take two of your beliefs that you hold or that hold you back. They may be very general or very specific - 'All politicians are power crazed and self-centred,' or 'My boss hates me and always tries to find fault with what I do,' or 'All Englishmen are arrogant snobs.'

Write out what the opposite beliefs would be. Now define your new comfort zones and self-talk. Consider what it would be like to hold these new beliefs. How would your behaviour and results change?

Belief 1	Belief 2
Opposite Belief 1	Opposite Belief 2
New Comfort Zone 1	New Comfort Zone 2
New Self-talk 1	New Self-talk 2
New Belief 1	New Belief 2
New Behaviour/Result 1	New Behaviour/Result 2

Challenging Our Beliefs

Identify a situation where you are making a judgement about a person, an action, a behaviour or some spoken words.

What thoughts go through your mind when you first come into that situation?	
What feelings does the situation generate in you?	
What do you say to yourself in this situation?	
What are the judgements that you make about this situation – the person, or the behaviour?	
How do you react to the situation – how do you express your thoughts, feelings and judgements?	

Now go deeper and explore the beliefs that lie behind your thoughts, feelings and judgements. To do this you need to detach yourself from the situation and see it as though you are a spectator.

What are the different intentions that could lie behind the person's behaviour or words? Do you know what they are? Or or are you guessing?	
How much of your judgement comes from the projection of your own thoughts, feelings and intentions?	
What is the belief on which your judgement is based, and where does this come from (parents, school, national culture, etc.)?	
What would happen if I changed that belief? How would I react to the person/ behaviour now? What would be the impact of changing?	
Do I want to keep, change or get rid of this belief pattern?	

PHYSICAL FITNESS

All is one. It makes sense, then, that our physical, spiritual, mental and emotional states all impact on each other. I know that there is much research on those links, but this has been my own experience – and that is what motivates me to maintain my physical fitness. There are other factors.

The Impact of Fitness

I enjoy being fit. I enjoy the process of getting and being fit. It wasn't an especially enlightened decision. I remember deciding, when I was a podgy, 13-year-old, not to be fat because James Bond said 'One should never get fat' in one of the Fleming books. I admit that my fantasy was to be like James Bon,d and I have happily let my physical fitness regime become a habit, perhaps even an obsession over the years. I have become extremely sensitive to my physical condition and, importantly, how it impacts on my mind, my emotions and sense of self. My posture, the shoes I wear and how I move and feel the ground in them, my suppleness and lack of it all affect me.

One experiment I conducted as part of my postgraduate studies in spiritual facilitation was to study the impact of me smiling more. It was fascinating to see the reaction in other people and within myself. Now I understand how the act of using the muscles involved in smiling impacts on the part of the brain controlling our feelings of happiness and wellbeing. Now I understand how we all react instinctively to facial expressions – and we mirror the feelings they represent. How we stand or sit impacts on our emotional state and on the perceptions of those around us. The body and the mind are separate and yet, at the same time, one whole. Our self and others are separate and yet, at the same time, one whole.

Mind, emotions, body and spirit, the energies of the chakras – they are all part of the 'whole' that we call self. Physical fitness in all its forms, and the discipline and effort required in developing it, enhance my sense of self-worth and emotional state, they impact on my mental sharpness and it has become a spiritual practice – caring for the 'temple of my soul'.

Lessons for Life

Fitness training and the sporting arena also provides a way of developing mental and emotional resilience and mastery. The principles of true sportsmanship provide a code of behaviour which is then tested as we unleash our instinctive, competitive and, often, violent nature against others. Playing to win at the same time as playing with honour and within the spirit of sport is a great challenge and a forge for our base metal.

Because your strength, energy and condition vary from day to day, season to season, and from age to age, this means that you should also regulate their exercise to meet your own needs. When you are young and in the prime life, doing strenuous physical exercises is appropriate. However, I am told that as one ages, one's exercise can and should become milder and less strenuous. Exercise which results in a person feeling exhausted afterwards is too much. Find your own path – I still love to push myself through a certain amount of pain and feel a level of exhaustion.

Let me outline the different kinds of exercise that you can build into your own fitness regime – your Wheel of Life.

Life Itself

In economically richer countries, many of the simple physical tasks have been replaced by machines and appliances. So, in such countries, one of the easiest ways of getting adequate exercise is, wherever possible, to leave the car, the lift or escalator and other

175

mechanical conveniences. Instead of driving everywhere, sometimes one should walk or ride their bicycle. Instead of taking the lift, one should walk up the stairs. This kind of exercise is relatively easy to do since it is purposeful and uncontrived.

Breathing

One hugely neglected exercise is breathing. Yes, breathing. We never get taught to breathe – we just do it, automatically, every single moment of our lives. Yes, but this simple act provides us with the oxygen that is the source of our energy, of our life. I have a book called *Anapanasati* which means mindful breathing. A whole book. So there is much to discover, but one simple practice right now is to take just two or three minutes three times a day to breathe deeply – inhaling for six seconds, holding for two seconds, exhaling for seven seconds. Begin each breath by pushing out your abdomen so that you have the feeling of breathing deep down to the base of your spine. Just notice the impact it has on your mind, on your emotions and on your body. Try that same exercise when you are getting agitated or stressed and notice the impact it has on your emotions then. When you meditate, focus on the breath and what it means to you. The Latin word for breath is *spiritum*, the root of our word 'spirit'. Learning how to breathe can have a profound impact on our lives.

Stamina

Some people just cannot find the time get their exercise entirely by doing manual chores during their daily schedule. In that case, it is necessary to set time aside to deliberately exercise. There are three types of exercise a person should do to stay healthy. The first of these is aerobic exercise. This means doing something fast enough and repetitive enough to get one's heart beating faster than normal. There are different ways to use aerobic exercise – the high intensity training increases the aerobic-anaerobic threshold and the lower intensity work develops our fat-burning capability. The exact rate will depend on your age, current physical condition and normal pulse rate.

The low intensity rates can be accomplished by fast walking, jogging, riding a bicycle, swimming, playing basketball or any number of other methods of exertion. The aim is to keep that heart rate raised for 30 to 40 minutes. The important thing is that whatever method of exercise one chooses should not cause any damage to your body. Since many types of aerobic exercise consist of repetitive movements, if they are even just a little bit damaging to the joints and tendons, a host of small injuries may accumulate to cause a large problem. So, choose an aerobic activity which will not result in cumulative stress injuries or vary the activity so as not to always stress the same body parts.

I have had to change my routine over the years. When I left the army, my knees and back were 'shot'. I tried to keep running for a few more years, change my running style, using 'barefoot' shoes, but the stress was transferred from my knees to my calf muscles and ankle tendons. Now, I have moved to the cross-trainers in the gym and cycling, with the low impact being far better for my knees and back.

Aerobic exercise results in better circulation of blood and body fluids. It strengthens the heart and lungs and reduces the negative effects of stress and emotional strain. The general guidance is for young and middle-aged people to do some kind of aerobic activity at least three times per week. I have to force myself to have a rest day every few days – so, find what works for you.

Strength – Resistance Training

Resistance training refers to lifting or pushing against something heavy or difficult to move. Resistance training builds physical strength. Lifting weights, doing push-ups, sit-ups, and pull-ups, or

177

using any of the numerous types of resistance training machines on the market, can help convert fatty tissue into muscle. Muscle burns more calories than does adipose or fatty tissue. Not only will this result in a slimmer, trimmer body, but you will also feel mentally and emotionally good about your renewed physical strength. The old saying goes, 'Nothing succeeds like success.' I allow myself some narcissism to maintain my fitness. I use a healthy pride and positive self-image to help develop more *joie de vivre* and with that a longer, healthier life.

When you get to 40 years of age your metabolism naturally slows down with the associated decline of organ functions. Practically speaking, this results in gaining approximately 10 pounds of fat every decade after that age, unless you take preventive steps. After 40, you will gain weight even if you eat the same amounts and kinds of foods and get the same amount of exercise you did before that age. In other words, to counteract this process, you must do more and/or eat less than you did before. I know this from painful, lasting experience. The good news is that, if you are prepared to put the work in, that decline doesn't have to happen. I am the same weight now as I was in my rugby-playing days 40 years ago.

When doing resistance training, you should exercise all major muscle groups. Don't try to build huge muscles – unless you are entering a Mr or Miss Universe competition – but rather concentrate on toning and firming what you have. This usually means lighter weights or less resistance and more repetitions. Resistance training can be done three or more times per week but should be done at least twice a week. Besides the benefits mentioned above, resistance training also results in stronger bones and tendons.

Stretching

Stretching exercises help to loosen the joints and promote the free flow of *energy* and blood over the channels and connecting vessels. They strengthen the tendons and ligaments and indirectly strengthen the bones. Further, stretching exercises help promote mental and physical relaxation.

Stretching exercises are easiest to do in the late afternoon or early evening, and are hardest to do in the early morning when you first wake up. However, doing stretching exercises in the morning helps to free the flow of *qi* and blood which has become sluggish overnight. When doing stretching exercises, it is important to relax into each stretch. One should work with their breath, relaxing further with each exhalation. One should not try to stretch by bouncing into a stretch, nor should they force themselves to stretch too far too fast. Rather, one should stretch little by little, day by day, making haste slowly.

The most important stretches are to flex and extend the spine, to adduct the spine, and to rotate the spine. Also, one should stretch out the backs of the legs, which tend to be tight. One can also stretch their legs apart as if attempting a split. Stretching should be a daily practice to keep the body supple, allow the blood to flow freely, and the mind relaxed.

Sports

As well as providing exercise, sport has other benefits. Sport is a vehicle for physical, emotional and mental development. It can encourage self-awareness, personal and team discipline, determination and focus. All sports can teach what it takes to be part of a team and how to compete fairly; to win and to lose with dignity.

Sport provides a channel for our competitive, often violent instinctive nature. It can help us to learn how to control that nature, developing emotional maturity and mental resilience. It can help to develop positive values, self-discipline and a respect for others around us, a responsibility for our behaviour and the choices we make.

Sport is a bridge between nations and communities and forges friendships that break through the social barriers that divide our world. It can provide a common sense of purpose, strong, shared values and a common language.

> *'Sport has the power to change the world. It has the power to inspire. It has the power to unite people in a way that little else does. It speaks to youth in a language they understand. Sport can create hope where once there was only despair. It is more powerful than government in breaking down racial barriers.' Nelson Mandela*

Sport is normally a separate element on the curriculum and yet there are so many lessons that can be learnt from even the simplest of sporting activities, training sessions, games or events.

Qi Gong

Qi Gong means 'energy with skill'. It's an ancient Chinese practice designed to enhance the flow of chi or energy in and around our physical bodies. It is based on an understanding of our nature as human and living beings – drawn from what has come to be known as 'eastern philosophy'. This philosophy has gained acceptance in the west as our modern sciences have also moved us towards an understanding that we are dynamic, interwoven energy systems rather than separate mechanisms.

Although many martial art practitioners use it to focus their energy or develop suppleness and sensitivity, Qi Gong is a practice in its own right. It encourages good physical health, vitality and develops inner power. It helps in curing illness, developing emotional balance and resilience, mental strength, youthfulness and spiritual cultivation.

Qi Gong consists of many thousands of breathing, movement and meditational exercises that help enhance the flow of energy. It's this flow, this 'living in harmony with', that is a vital part of the disciplines of both Qi Gong and also Tai Chi. As a stagnant pond becomes silted and a source of disease, and a fast flowing stream brings vigour, freshness and purity, so it is with our mind and body. As a stick or branch held too rigidly can be broken and the green, flexible bamboo survives, so it is with our mind and body. Qi Gong encourages flexibility and flow in both body and mind.

Qi Gong should be practised within the physical limits of your own body - one should not overstretch or burden joints and ligaments. But each exercise should be completed with discipline as well as lightness; each exercise is a mental as well as physical discipline.

As we age, we do not need and indeed should not do the heavy exercise we were capable of as a young or middle-aged adult. Qi Gong exercises are a way of getting moderate exercise without excessive strain. As middle age gives way to old age, it is probably better for most people to combine Qi Gong with stretching exercises and then to be sure they stay physically active in their daily routine.

Although one must moderate their exercise with advancing age, it is nonetheless important not to stop exercising. One of the characteristics of chi within the human body is movement. The body stops moving when the chi departs. But if one stops moving, one's chi will depart all the quicker.

Qi Gong – Body, Mind and Spirit

What I love about Qi Gong and Tai Chi is that they are not just physical exercise. They are the physical expression of a rich philosophy and deeper mental and physical practices. There are three aspects in all types of Qi Gong; the form, energy and mind. If you practise only the form or the movement, without the energy and the mind dimensions, then you are merely performing a physical, stretching exercise. For an effective control of energy, you have to enter a state of mind called 'entering zen' or 'entering silence'. When you are in zen or a meditative state of mind, you can, among other things, tap energy from the cosmos and direct the energy to flow to wherever you want in your body.

Tai Chi

Old men moving gracefully in the park. The Chinese workforce exercising in harmony before the day's work begins. Maybe these are images that appear when we hear the words Tai Chi.

> 'Tai Chi Chuan is a Chinese martial art and exercise method – and a great deal more besides ...' *Dan Docherty*

Tai Chi means 'Supreme Ultimate' and Tai Chi Chuan (chuan meaning 'fist') is an ancient Chinese martial art. The origins are clouded in the mists of time and argued over by historians and the students of the various Ta Chi schools, for it has a rich history of myths, masters, schools and many forms.

Like Qi Gong, the art of Tai Chi is based on Eastern philosophy and an acknowledgement of the importance of living in harmony with the natural rhythm of the universe rather than in conflict. For this reason it is known as a 'soft' martial art. It becomes more attractive in the west as we become more aware of the impact we have had and are having on each other and the environment through our desire to impose on each other rather than live in harmony. It is part of the mythology that the moves of Tai Chi were based on observations of a fight between a snake and a crane – strike, counter-strike, never over-extending and always responding to the energy of the other. It is this natural rhythm that lies at the heart of Tai Chi.

The practise of the defence movements, which are joined together into what is known as the 'form', is a good physical exercise, but it also disciplines the mind. The movements enhance the flow of chi or energy, and that flow becomes a form of meditation, bringing emotional and mental balance and peace. It is a practical self-defence form with principles that can be seen reflected in Sun Tzu's *Art of War* but it also brings to life many aspects of the Tao Te Ching, Buddhism and Confucianism.

Tai Chi also encourages contemplation on the 'way' (Tao) you live your life, it helps you to manage your emotions and focus your thoughts and actions. To become skilled in Tai Chi requires an awareness of self, an awareness and sensitivity to others and the 'right' application of Yin and Yang to any situation. Tai Chi, for me, reflects the journey of personal mastery.

There are many different forms of Tai Chi Chuan and many levels of training and development. There are many teachers too, and I recommend that, if you would like to explore Tai Chi, you work with different teachers until you find one that suits you and what you are seeking.

LEARNING JOURNAL

The journal is a space for your own thoughts and feelings, for your dreams and fears, for the lessons you learn and the promises you make. There is no right or wrong way to record your experiences; it can be a cathartic process where you can let off steam, or a space for creative writing or drawing. The formats on this page are examples of how you might structure your thinking - but I suggest that you treat yourself to a beautiful empty book to capture your thoughts.

Journal Entry for a Specific Event

The Event or Activity

My Experience
(Thoughts, feelings, actions and reactions, observations of others)

Feedback from Others

What Lessons Can I Draw from This Experience?
(Lessons that are relevant to me, to my team or organisation)

What Actions Will I Take to Apply These Lessons?
(What will I do, how and when?)

Journal Entry for A Day/Week/Month

Day/Date – Time Period

Reflections

Insights/Lessons

Actions for tomorrow

Checklist:

Physical (Sleep, energy, exercise)   Emotional (Moods, interactions)
Intellectual (lessons, knowledge)   Spiritual (Balance, wellbeing, insights)

Annex C

MY PATH

The Meaning of Life

The Guiding Principles

WHO AM I?

My Purpose

THE DIMENSIONS OF MY SELF

This exercise is an important stage on the inner journey. It is a reflection on the many dimensions of the dynamic energy system that is our self. As you spend time on each dimension, you will see how they all impact on each other. You will also see how the inner world impacts on the outer.

In our relationships, many of the judgements that we make on the behaviour of others are based on our own inner thoughts, feelings, prejudices and experiences. There are times when we will transfer our thoughts and feelings about a person or experience onto another person who currently fills a related role. As an example, all our previous thoughts and feelings about authority figures may be transferred onto the person who we currently see playing that 'authority role'.

As we work on our inner world, we can become more aware of the impact of the outer world. Many of these influences work at the unconscious level - we are not aware of them or where they come from. They have merged into our sense of identity and we can find it very difficult to accept a challenge to their validity or relevance. Our thinking is coloured by national, ethnic and family influences. It will be touched too, by our religion or faith. This is an opportunity to take back control of your own thinking and feeling.

Healing Through Meditation, Colour and Sound

We may have never experienced a deep sense of connection through our heart centre or a sense of our own deep intuition.

There are ways, through meditation, that you can develop the energy in these different dimensions. Meditate on the colour of the chakra or dimension that you want to work on. Wear the colour that represents the energy you want more of in your life. Visualise breathing in the colour, or breathing into that centre.

It will be an interesting part of your journey, to notice the opening of these energy centres within you.

Inspiration
Our sense of purpose and
meaning in our work and life

Intuition
Our sense of rightness and of
'knowing'

I-Expression
Our ability to express our whole
self - the creative talents

Interconnection
An awareness of the unity of all
life - leading to a sense of service

Intellect
The little I or ego, sense of self-
esteem and our mental ability

Intimacy
Our emotional intelligence and
ability to develop relationships
with the world around us

Instinct
Our drive for achievement, for
survival, to win. Our physical
energy and will.

How am I doing in each area? What is left to do?

MY GUIDING VALUES

MY PERSONAL CODE

MY PERSONAL VISION

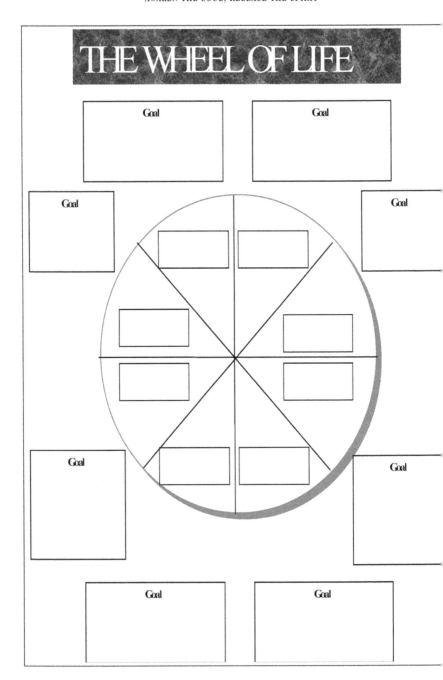

Roles	Purpose/Goal	Objectives to Achieve the Goal	Actions Transfer to Diary

MY PLANS, PRACTICES AND COMMITMENTS

Practice	Purpose	Goals/Objectives and Timings (R	Actions Transfer to Diary

My Schedule

Daily Practices	Time/Duration

Weekly Practices	Time/Duration

Monthly/Quarterly/Annual Practices	Time/Duration

The Next Stage of the Journey

I hope that you have enjoyed my words. I hope that you choose to explore more of your own spiritual impulse and find your own path to peace and harmony.

I talked about the loneliness of this path and I have appreciated the friends and teachers who have supported me on my journey. I would like to offer that same support to you. You can contact me through my website.

Chalybeate Healing

www.chalybeatehealing.com

To explore how you might contribute to the quest to bring more light and love into the world, you might be interested in my charity work at

Small Acts of Kindness

www.saok.org.uk

I hope that our paths may cross and we may walk together on the mountain.

Lightning Source UK Ltd.
Milton Keynes UK
UKHW010702150921
390602UK00001B/25

*Awaken
the Soul,
Release
the Spirit*